VANCOUVER ISLAND
BOOK OF
Everything

Everything you wanted to know about
Vancouver Island and were going
~~to~~ ask anyway

t, Suzanne Morphet
and Diane Selkirk

MACINTYRE PURCELL PUBLISHING INC.

MacIntyre Purcell Publishing Inc.
232 Lincoln St., Suite D
PO Box 1142
Lunenburg, Nova Scotia
B0J 2C0
(902) 640-3350
www.bookofeverything.com
info@bookofeverything.com

Cover photo courtesy: Tourism Vancouver Island
istockphoto: page 6, 8, 20, 34, 44, 56, 78, 94, 118, 144, 160, 192

Printed and bound in Canada.

Library and Archives Canada Cataloguing in Publication
Grant, Peter, 1948-
Vancouver Island Book of Everything: everything you wanted to
know about Vancouver Island and were going to ask anyway / Peter
Grant, Suzanne Morphet and Diane Selkirk.

ISBN 978-0-9784784-8-3
1. Vancouver Island (B.C.) 2. Vancouver Island (B.C.)--Miscellanea.
I. Morphet, Suzanne II. Selkirk, Diane III. Title.
FC3844.42.G73 2008   971.1'2
C2008-903309-4

Introduction

The title hooked me. *Book of Everything*. Concise reference books about Canadian cities and provinces. Brilliant. There was to be one about Vancouver Island, my home and native land. It was to be the first Book of Everything about a region and I wanted in.

To those who live on this very big island and the smaller islands around it, it is a place apart. It's a region with its own identity. Its own cultures. Its own rich history. And now — its own Book of Everything.

The intention is first, to depict the islands as they are right now, today, and second, to trace *the historical arc* (invoking a favorite phrase of the publisher). The historical arc is important because by the time you read these words, almost certainly some of the facts and numbers will already be out of date.

We hope the *Vancouver Island Book of Everything* brings the clarity of a snapshot to the life of the islands. From my own perspective, it's the picture of a society that is turning the corner to sustainable economies, sustainable communities and sustainable cultures.

We put great effort into locating the latest, most relevant information, taking stock of the island's strengths and weaknesses both. When one looks at the dizzying economic and social developments of the last 30 years — not all of them good — it helps to remember that some residents view the life of the island through the prism of five or more millennia.

I would like to thank writer Suzanne Morphet who contributed the Timeline, Weather, Place Names and Then and Now and to Diane Selkirk who contributed research to the book. Thanks also to editor Kelly Inglis. Thanks especially to the many people who contributed special knowledge about the islands in the Take 5 personal compilations, and so many others who willingly shared information and perspective.

Publisher John MacIntyre has been both cheerleader and taskmaster to this project. One could not wish for a more encouraging cheerleader or a more politely persistent taskmaster.

— Peter Grant

Table of Contents

Somewhere On The Island

Gary Fjellgaard is the cowboy singer-songwriter of Gabriola Island. His song here captures something about these islands that has eluded some great writers. A native of Saskatchewan, Fjellgaard logged in northern BC before taking up a career in music. Over nearly 40 years he has earned many accolades in folk and country circles.

Look at all these Islands
Granite walls and sandstone
See the mighty evergreens
Standing by the shore
How those waves have pounded
Down thru the ages
Somewhere thru eternity
Gone for evermore

I can hear a heartbeat somewhere on the ocean
Somewhere on the changing tide
I can hear the wind so wild shouting cross the sand
I can hear an eagle screaming of an eagle
Somewhere in the distant sky
I hear somebody cryin someone softly cryin
Somewhere on the Island

Look at all the old men
Watered eyed and shakin
Still dreamin bout the olden days
Behind their mystic door
When they lived upon the Island
And never made a footprint
They just barely touched their moccasins
Upon the forest floor

Someone said that's progress
Someone said destruction
Someone said that I don't really care
I just don't give a damn
Look at all the children
Trust upon their faces
Hoping for a legacy
Untouched by foolish hands

Publisher: Slim Creek Music

Vancouver Island:

A Timeline

380 million years ago: Formation of the earliest rocks found on Vancouver Island and nearby Salt Spring Island. The islands are created over aeons by a combination of metamorphosis, tectonic movement, erosion, sedimentation, molten flows from volcanoes, glacial scrapings and deposits.

8,000 years ago: Aboriginal peoples settle on the north Pacific coast.

1774: Captain Juan Perez of Spain is the first European to discover Vancouver Island and trade with the local Nuu-chah-nulth people from his ship. The Spanish make three more expeditions to the coast between 1775 and 1779, claiming the land for Spain.

1778: English navigator Captain James Cook anchors in Nootka Sound while searching for the Northwest Passage. He becomes the first white man to set foot on the island.

1779: A smallpox epidemic, likely introduced by the Spanish expedition of Juan Francisco de la Bodega y Quadra, devastates the First Nations population.

1787: Frances Trevor Barkley, wife of Captain Charles Barkley, is the first European woman to set foot on Vancouver Island.

1789: Spanish Captain Estéban José Martinez seizes several British ships at Nootka Sound for trading in territory claimed by Spain. The incident almost starts a war between the two countries. The Spanish build Fort San Miguel on a small offshore island, while English trader John Meares claims to have bought land from Nuuu-chah-nulth Chief Maquinna.

1790: Spain and Britain sign the Nootka Convention, with Spain giving up any rights to the island.

1792: Two Spanish schooners make the first continuous circumnavigation of Vancouver Island, joined part way by Captain George Vancouver.

1792: Captain George Vancouver and Spanish Captain Juan Francisco de la Bodega y Quadra's meet at Friendly Cove, Nootka Sound and agree to name the island Quadra's and Vancouver's Island.

1824: Formal correspondence from the Hudson's Bay Company (HBC) refers to the island as Vancouver's Island.

1843: The HBC fort known variously as Fort Albert, Fort Victoria and Fort Camosun was renamed Fort Victoria in a special ceremony with gun salutes.

1846: Oregon Boundary Treaty, also called the Treaty of Washington, establishes the 49th parallel as the boundary between American and British territories in the west.

1849: The Colony of Vancouver Island is created by royal charter and the HBC is leased to the entire island for seven shillings a year, on condition that the colony succeed. Richard Blanshard is named as the first governor in March 1850.

Bio THE MAN BEHIND THE NAME

George Vancouver was a man with a mission, or, more precisely, two missions. In 1791, he was tasked with charting the west coast of North America from northern California to Alaska; and secondly he was also tasked with settling damages on behalf of Britain from Spanish seizure of three British ships at Nootka Sound in 1789.

On the first task, Vancouver and his crew proved themselves to be worthy cartographers (Vancouver had learned the skills under James Cook), producing comprehensive charts of the west coast and proving once and for all there was no Northwest Passage, south of 65° N. Vancouver's charts of Northwest America were so accurate that they were used as a reference for coastal navigation for more than 140 years.

He was less successful in carrying out the second task. At Nootka Sound, Vancouver met Spanish captain Juan Francisco de la Bodega y Quadra, and though they couldn't make diplomatic headway, they struck up a personal friendship. Vancouver enjoyed the Spanish captain's company so much that he suggested that Quadra's name precede his own in naming the island, and for some years thereafter the island was called Quadra's and Vancouver's Island.

When Vancouver returned to England, his ships had completed the longest (4½ years) survey expedition in history. As he wrote his 4-volume Voyages, his troubles mounted. Already ill, he came under attack by influential associates and shipboard subordinates for his leadership, particularly his temperamental outbursts and harsh punishments. He died at the age of 40 in 1798. Vancouver's brother saw to it the account of his remarkable survey was published. Vancouver's astounding thoroughness and accuracy, comparable to that of James Cook, the Great Navigator himself, has far outshone his glaring defects of character.

1851: James Douglas becomes second Governor of Vancouver Island, after Richard Blanshard resigns, citing poor health and lack of compensation. Douglas keeps his HBC position as well.

1851: Thomas and Ann Blinkhorn and family and James Cooper arrive on the *Tory* — Vancouver Island's first settlers independent of the HBC. They establish a farm in Metchosin.

1852: Coal is discovered in present day Nanaimo and the HBC creates a settlement there called Colviletown.

1852: Victoria townsite is laid out in streets.

1854: After the outbreak of the Crimean War, the Royal Navy starts using Esquimalt Harbour, and in 1865 establishes its Pacific headquarters there.

1858: Gold is discovered on the Fraser River, and as many as 30,000 miners descend on Victoria, population less than 1,000, to obtain permits and supplies.

1858: The Colony of British Columbia is formed on the mainland. James Douglas is appointed Governor, continuing as well as Governor of the Colony of Vancouver Island.

1859: The 'Birdcages' — the first colonial Parliament Buildings — are built in Victoria.

1860: Fisgard Lighthouse is built at the entrance to Esquimalt Harbour to warn ships approaching the Royal Navy Base.

1862: A case of smallpox, most likely arriving with the goldseekers, hits the shores of the island. The outbreak spreads through the First

Nations encampment around Victoria, and when the visitors flee to their homes, it spreads up the coast as far as Alaska. About one-third of north Pacific coast First Nations populations die in the epidemic.

1862: The colony's first gas lights are lit in Victoria. Victoria becomes the second incorporated city in BC; Thomas Harris is elected its first mayor.

1864: Gold is discovered on the Sooke River by Lieutenant Peter Leech, for which Leechtown was named. The rush lasts about a year.

Take 5 BARB WHITTINGTON'S FAVOURITE
MEMORIES OF GROWING UP

Barbara Helem Whittington was born and raised in Port Alberni. Even today she considers the Alberni Valley as a haven of civilization on an uncivilized island. A resident of Central Saanich with three grown sons, she is a professor in the School of Social Work at the University of Victoria.

1. Once a year the lakes around Port Alberni would freeze, and Dad would take us up to the Hump to skate on Dog Lake and Loon Lake.

2. Living in a small town, we could walk to meet our friends. You'd phone to say you were on your way.

3. Dad was a doctor. He'd call to say he had a couple of house calls and would be home soon, and I'd sit on the porch and watch for him. He'd move over and let me drive. Even when he was exhausted he'd play with us.

4. Family holidays, when you packed up the car so that it would barely hold everything, and you'd take off, not knowing what would happen or even where you'd go — maybe to Long Beach on the twisty, windy logging roads.

5. Being able to stay at our cabin on Sproat Lake without adults. We were trusted — big mistake. We'd take the boat out in the middle of the night to see where the parties were. We just pointed the boat toward the most noise.

1864: James Douglas, the Father of British Columbia, retires as governor of the two colonies and is replaced by two governors, one in Victoria and the other in New Westminster. Douglas is knighted.

1866: An Act is passed by the Imperial Parliament, which combines the colonies of Vancouver Island and British Columbia into one colony now called British Columbia. New Westminster is named as the capital.

1867: The first of two petitions is circulated by Americans living in Victoria proposing the colony be annexed to the United States. The petition receives little support but serves to accelerate demand for BC to join Canada.

1868: After much political haggling, a vote in the BC legislature supports Victoria as the colony's capital.

1871: British Columbia becomes the sixth province to join the Dominion of Canada; the Federal government promises a railway within 10 years.

1871: Emily Carr is born in Victoria's James Bay neighbourhood. She will become Canada's most famous female artist acknowledged as one of the greatest women in art, and win a Governor General's award for her writing.

1877: James Dunsmuir builds and operates BC's first telephones, between Wellington and Departure Bay, using designs published in *Scientific American Magazine*.

1878: Sir John A. Macdonald is defeated in his home riding and is parachuted into Victoria where he wins a seat in Parliament in a by-election.

1882: Victoria gets electric streetlights (a first in BC). Arc lamps mounted on three tall poles were powered by a 25 hp steam engine.

1885: Canada introduces a $50 head tax on every Chinese person entering the country. This leads to smuggling and the construction of secret passageways in Victoria's Chinatown.

1885: Businessman Francis Barnard begins a scheduled 'bus' service (between 8 am and 8 pm) on two routes in Victoria with horses and buggies.

1890: Victoria is the 3rd city in Canada with streetcars.

1890: Victoria's magnificent Craigdarroch Castle, built by coal baron Robert Dunsmuir, is completed months after his death.

1897-1898: A gold rush in the Klondike River, Yukon Territory, induces an economic boom in Victoria and other port cites as prospectors are required to purchase a year's supplies.

1898: The new BC Parliament Buildings, designed by Francis Rattenbury, open in Victoria, having cost $923,000, almost double the budget.

1908: The CPR Empress Hotel opens in Victoria.

1912: Victoria defeats New Westminster 5 to 1 in the first professional hockey game to be played on the Pacific coast.

1912-1914: The Great Strike, one of Canada's longest and most violent labour disputes.

1921: Work begins on Canada's largest dry dock, in Esquimalt.

1922: Drivers on the island switch from driving on the left hand side to the right.

1925: The Victoria Cougars win the Stanley Cup, beating the Montreal Canadiens 3 games to 1.

1942: A Japanese submarine surfaces about three kilometres off Estevan Point on the island's west coast and fires 25 rounds at the lighthouse. If this disputed claim is true, it was the only time Canada was under attack in either world war.

1956: 18-year-old Marilyn Bell becomes the first woman and the youngest person to swim the Strait of Juan de Fuca. She swam the 29-km-wide strait in 11 hours 35 minutes.

1958: Ripple Rock in Seymour Narrows near Campbell River is blown up to make safer passage for boats. The blast is one of the world's largest non-nuclear explosions.

1960: BC Ferries begins service with two ships and two terminals, one at Swartz Bay, the other at Tsawwassen.

1962: The Trans-Canada highway officially opens, with 14 cars completing an 8,000 km journey from St. John's, Newfoundland to Victoria.

1963: Victoria College is reborn as the University of Victoria.

1968: The first high-voltage direct-current (HVDC) transmission line in North America is energized between Ladner on the mainland and Duncan on Vancouver Island.

1980: The idea for a fixed link to the mainland is first studied.

1981: BC Hydro tests a vertical axis wind turbine on southern Vancouver Island.

Cougar Annie

Willie Rae-Arthur loved the booze and was a frequent visitor at the opium dens of Vancouver's Chinatown — not very becoming for a married father of three. The family was always broke, despite the money his rich Scottish sister sent every month. To get him away from temptation and keep the remittances coming, they moved to the west coast of Vancouver Island.

Willie and Ada Annie Rae-Arthur arrived in Boat Basin, an isolated reach at the north end of Clayoquot Sound, in 1915. They preempted 160 acres, built a cabin and, in 1923, a house. They had eight more children. Ada Annie cleared 5 acres and started a garden and orchard.

Eventually she sold seeds and bulbs by mail order, using the mail service of the CPR coastal steamer *Princess Maquinna*. She ran a general store out of her home. Her vegetables were always in demand. Ada Annie was a crack shot and became known for taking down dozens of cougars that would pick off their sheep and goats.

Willie is remembered as a lively conversationalist and a bit of a poet who would row to Tofino — a day's trip each way — to be with his cronies. After Willie's death, "Cougar Annie" became postmistress of the new Boat Basin Post Office. She lived in Boat Basin for 3 husbands and nearly 5 decades more.

A new chapter of the story began after Ada Annie's death in 1985, at the age of 97. A retired stockbroker from Vancouver bought the property and began to reclaim the garden. Today it is owned by the Boat Basin Foundation, which operates a field centre for rainforest research. It's billed as the only pioneer homestead in Clayoquot Sound remaining in private hands, and the only garden "of this scope" on the west coast. The foundation offers tours by arrangement.

1982: Haida, islanders' favourite whale, dies in captivity at Sealand of the Pacific in Oak Bay. The death occurs only a few days before he was to be released back in to the wild.

1985: Canada and the US sign the Pacific Salmon Treaty to help better manage and share salmon stocks.

1993: Over 12,000 people protest the logging of old growth forests in Clayoquot Sound, leading to the largest mass arrest in Canadian history. More than 900 people are jailed, and 850 convicted of criminal contempt.

1994: The 15th Commonwealth Games are held in Victoria in August, hosting 63 nations.

1999: MacMillan Bloedel, BC's largest forest company, is sold to American timber giant Weyerhaeuser.

1999: A dilapidated fishing boat carrying 123 smuggled Chinese immigrants is intercepted by the Coast Guard near Gold River.

2000: Clayoquot Sound is designated a World Biosphere Reserve by UNESCO.

2005: BC Hydro drops plans for a 262-megawatt natural gas power plant at Duke Point. The project ran into opposition from environmentalists, industrial ratepayers and residents of Nanaimo.

2007: The *Titanic* exhibit at the Royal BC Museum draws a record crowd of 451,120 people over six months, and generates more than $30 million dollars in spending by visitors.

2008: Islanders join with other BC residents to celebrate the 150th anniversary of the founding of the Crown Colony of British Columbia.

2008: The Coastal Renaissance, the newest addition to the BC Ferries fleet, begins service between Departure Bay and Horseshoe Bay.

Vancouver Island Essentials

Origin of the Name: Vancouver Island was named after Royal Navy Captain George Vancouver, who surveyed the northwest coast of America between 1792 and 1794 and claimed it for the British monarch.

Entry into Canada: 1871 (as part of British Columbia)

Time Zone: Pacific Standard (GMT −8)

Area Code: 250

Postal Codes: V8K to V9Z

System of Measurement: Metric

Driving Age: 16

Voting Age: 18

Legal Drinking Age: 19

Statutory Holidays: New Years Day, Good Friday, Victoria Day, Canada Day, British Columbia Day, Labour Day, Thanksgiving Day, Remembrance Day and Christmas Day. (Easter Sunday, Easter Monday and Boxing Day are not.)

POPULATION IN PERSPECTIVE

Vancouver Island's population of 745,165 (2007) is more than 5 times that of Prince Edward Island (population 135,851) and 1½ times that of Newfoundland (island population 479,105). Vancouver Island's population accounts for 18 percent of the total British Columbia population and 2.3 percent of Canada's. Vancouver Island's growth rate was 0.9 percent in 2007, and the projected population in 2036 is expected to reach 920,282.

Residents are concentrated along the lowlands of the southeast coast. The six largest cities are there; they account for 82 percent of the total population found on the island. Nearly half the total population lives in Greater Victoria, the 15th largest metropolitan area in Canada. Nanaimo is the 38th largest in Canada. The population is increasing steadily in the southeast quarter — less rapidly than in the 90s — while many resource-based communities are losing population.

Source: Statistics Canada.

POPULATION DENSITY (PEOPLE/KM^2)

Vancouver Island: 22.4

British Columbia: 4.4

Canada: 3.5

Prince Edward Island: 23.9

Toronto: 3,939.4

New York City: 10,194.2

Take 5

BARBARA MCLINTOCK'S THINGS YOU DON'T KNOW ABOUT VANCOUVER ISLAND

Barbara McLintock is a coroner with the BC Coroner Service. She is also an author and retired journalist. She lives in Victoria.

1. People are welcome to take wedding pictures on the Legislature lawns, but there's a time limit of 1 1/2 hours, because the grounds can get crowded.
2. The chapel at St. Ann's Academy was deconsecrated in 1973. Once a month there is a traditional Catholic mass in Latin.
3. Saanich is the only place in North America where you can find Eurasian skylarks, the descendants of birds imported from England at the turn of the 20th century.
4. Spode, the famous English china works, made a set of china especially for the Butchart Gardens in 1937, with a floral motif, of course.
5. The Hudson's Bay Company named Beacon Hill in Beacon Hill Park. They kept two beacons burning at night so that shipmen could triangulate their position relative to Brotchie Ledge.

ON A TYPICAL DAY ON VANCOUVER ISLAND . . .

- 16 babies are born
- 19 people die
- 11 weddings occur
- 5 couples divorce

POPULATION BY AGE AND SEX

Median age: 43.8 years
Median age of men: 42; of women: 44
BC's median age: 40.2 years

Did you know...

that when an Islander says they are going "Up Island," they are going to any part of the island that is north of Victoria?

They Said It

"A great many canoes filled with the Natives were about the ships all day, and a trade commenced betwixt us and them, which was carried on with the Strictest honisty on boath sides. Their articles were the Skins of various animals, such as Bears, Wolfs, Foxes, Dear, Rackoons, Polecats, Martins and in particular the Sea Beaver, the same as is found on the coast of Kamtchatka."

– Captain James Cook's journal entry for March 30, 1778, during his third voyage exploring the Pacific Ocean, recording the first transactions for sea otter pelts with First Nations people of Vancouver Island.

LIFE AND DEATH

Life Expectancy: 81.1 years (2007)
Fertility Rate: 1,336 lifetime births per 1,000 women
Sex ratio: 956 males for every 1000 females

Source: BC Statistics.

MARRIAGE AND DIVORCE

- Vancouver Island's population aged 15 and over: 552,590
- Percentage of those who are married: 50
- Percentage who are single, never married: 29
- Percentage who are divorced: 10
- Percentage who are widowed: 7
- Percentage who are separated: 4
- Marriage rate (per 1,000 population) in BC: 5.3
- Marriage rate in Prince Edward Island, the highest: 6.0
- Marriage rate in Quebec, the lowest: 2.8
- Canada's marriage rate: 4.7
- Rate of divorce (per 100 marriages) in BC: 44.7
- Divorce rate in Quebec, the highest: 49.7
- Divorce rate in Prince Edward Island, the lowest: 27.3
- Canada's divorce rate: 38.3

Sources: BC Statistics and Statistics Canada.

Take 5 VANCOUVER ISLAND'S
LARGEST CITIES 2007 (POPULATION)

1. **Victoria** 350,240
2. **Nanaimo** 97,977
3. **Courtenay** 53,389
4. **Duncan** 43,954
5. **Campbell River** 38,390

Source: BC Statistics.

FAMILY STRUCTURE

- Total families on Vancouver Island: 190,430
- Married couples: 71.5 percent
- Female single parent: 13.0 percent
- Common-law couples: 12.5 percent
- Male single parent: 3.0 percent
- Families with children: 54.0 percent
- Families without children: 46.0 percent

Did you know...

that Vancouver Island accounts for 17.3 percent of all migration in British Columbia?

Take 5 TOP FIVE RELIGIOUS AFFILIATIONS
(PERCENTAGE OF TOTAL POPULATION)

1. **Protestant** 40.7
2. **No religion** 38.8
3. **Roman Catholic** 14.4
4. **Sikh** 1.0
5. **Buddhist** 0.9

Source: BC Statistics.

YOU KNOW YOU'RE FROM

- You consider anything less than 5°C freezing.
- You consider anything above 25°C way too hot.
- You start wearing shorts in January.
- You notice your lifestyle has become unaffordable.
- You take a Gravol before driving to Tofino.
- Your wedding invitation specifies potluck.
- You know Douglas fir from hemlock, balsam or spruce. By smell.
- You have no trouble pronouncing Ucluelet, Sooke, Tahsis, and Zeballos.
- You have no concept of humidity without precipitation.
- You've actually used your mountain bike on a mountain.
- You know that squirrels are just rats with fluffy tails, even though tourists think they're cute.
- You carry sunglasses and an umbrella at all times.
- If you really wanted to, you could snowboard, sail, golf, and bike all in the same day.
- You know the provincial flower is the dogwood.
- You're confused as to why Saskatchewan and Manitoba are part of Western Canada.
- You know more people who own boats than air conditioners.
- You think Atlantic salmon doesn't deserve the name salmon when compared to Pacific salmon.
- You consider a week with no rain to be "great weather."
- You have no problems drinking your tap water.
- You leave the island to see the rest of Canada, and you realize that there is nothing better to see.
- You have been lost in the woods on several occasions; you know you will be again; and you're okay with that.
- You've heard about "the big one" and you just couldn't care less.
- You know how scary it is to drive next to a loaded logging truck.

VANCOUVER ISLAND WHEN . . .

- You can recite the BC Ferries safety announcement by heart.
- You know that a "1.5 hour ferry" really means 3 hours. Time to get to the ferry, wait for the ferry, get on the ferry, eat in the buffet on the ferry, and then wait for the broken down VW in front of you to get off the ferry.
- You recognize April 20th as a good reason to celebrate.
- "The Bay Centre" just sounds wrong.
- Your life was dramatically impacted by the four feet of snow that fell during the Blizzard of '96..
- You remember Uforia and the Cheesecake Factory with a sense of nostalgia.
- A stroll through Mayfair Mall turns into an informal high school reunion.
- Your parka gets worn exactly one time a year — on your annual trek to the mountains.
- You have never spent money on curl enhancers for your hair.
- The peaches you had for breakfast are super fresh; you picked them from the tree on your front lawn.
- Your 3-bedroom, single bath bungalow is worth as much as a mansion just about anywhere else in Canada.
- You drank green tea long before it became trendy.
- Your commute involves a ferry ride.
- Your home has a recycling room.
- You carry baggies for picking up dog poo.
- You swim in the harbour on New Year's Day.
- You'd rather do it yourself.
- Your clothes all have SPF ratings.
- Conversation with another islander generates at least three points of view.
- You laugh out loud when you hear the words, 'fast ferries.'

ABORIGINAL MINORITIES ORIGINS (PERCENT OF TOTAL POPULATION)

- Vancouver Island's total Aboriginal: 6.6
- Multiple origins: 3.9
- First Nations: 2.5
- Métis: 0.2
- Inuit: 0.02

VISIBLE MINORITIES ORIGINS (PERCENT OF TOTAL POPULATION)

- Chinese: 2.2
- South Asian: 1.5
- Southeast Asian: 0.5
- Black: 0.5
- Japanese: 0.4
- Filipino: 0.4
- Latin American: 0.3
- Korean: 0.2
- Multiple origins: 0.1
- West Asian: 0.08
- Arab: 0.05

Source: BC Statistics.

Take 5 PATRICK DUNAE'S ESSENTIAL
READS ABOUT VANCOUVER ISLAND

Patrick Dunae was born and educated in Victoria. He teaches history at Vancouver Island University, Nanaimo and the University of Victoria and is editor of the Vancouver Island digital archive viHistory.ca.

1. **Clive Phillipps-Wolley, *One of the Broken Brigade* (1897)**. The hero of this cautionary tale is an English remittance man who is fleeced by American real-estate sharks, settles in a cabin on Shawnigan Lake and is (eventually) reunited with his sweetheart.

2. **S. W. Jackman, *Vancouver Island* (1972)**. A Victoria history professor and prolific author wrote this engaging account of the island's history, geography, flora and fauna for readers in the Old Country. It's now a tad quaint — "The trip from Swartz Bay to Tsawwassen takes one hour and forty minutes and is reasonable: $5.00 (£2) per automobile and $2.00 (80p) per passenger."

3. **Charles Lillard, *Seven Shillings a Year* (1986)**. A refreshingly non-academic history of Vancouver Island, with a great narrative line, by a shirt-sleeves poet and historian.

4. **Marilyn Bowering, *To All Appearances a Lady* (1989)**. In the 1950s, a retired marine pilot circumnavigates Vancouver Island with the ghost of an elderly Chinese woman, who recalls 1890s labour unrest, anti-Chinese sentiment and the plight of lepers. Haunting and evocative, with extraordinary historical detail.

5. **Arthur Mayse, *My Father, My Friend* (1993)**. A well-known outdoor columnist penned this pastoral memoir of growing up in Nanaimo after World War I. It's *A River Runs Through It* in an Island setting.

Did you know...

LANGUAGE

Of the total population, residents whose mother tongue is:

English	88.1 percent
French	1.6 percent
Non-official languages	9.6 percent

The Best of BC

The Encyclopedia of British Columbia's website lists "100 Best Things About BC." Among them are these Vancouver Island notables:

- **#3 Emily Carr's paintings:** born and raised in Victoria, Carr was inspired by nature and First Nations culture. A few works are in the Art Gallery of Greater Victoria.
- **#12 Bruce Hutchison's journalism:** A political columnist and editor-in-chief of both the *Victoria Daily Times* and *Vancouver Sun*, Hutchison's many books won three Governor General's Awards, and he was awarded the Order of Canada.
- **#15 Della Falls:** a gem of Strathcona Provincial Park, it is one of Canada's tallest waterfalls, cascading down 440 metres.
- **#20 Gulf Islands:** the sheltered waterways and charming coastlines of more than 200 islands and islets in Georgia Strait, off Vancouver Island's southeast coast.
- **#21 Nanaimo bars:** a type of chocolate no-bake square that is rumoured to have originated in the Vancouver Island town of the same name in the 1950s.

Did you know...

that Canada's defining "49th parallel" (49° N latitude) runs through the town of Ladysmith?

English and French	0.2 percent
English and a non-official language	0.4 percent
French and a non-official language	0.02 percent
English, French and a non-official language	0.02 percent
Neither English nor French	0.4 percent

- **#25 Butchart Gardens:** 20 hectares of floral finery on the Saanich Inlet estate of local cement magnate Robert Butchart and his wife Jenny, who created the Sunken Garden from an exhausted limestone quarry."
- **#34 Robson Bight:** a small bay on Vancouver Island's northeast coast where orca whales congregate to use the unique rubbing beach, which is protected in a BC ecological reserve.
- **#36 Whaler's Shrine:** Near the First Nations village of Yuquot (Friendly Cove), on Nootka Island, was a shrine where Mowachaht whalers went to cleanse and pray in preparation; since 1905, stored at the American Museum of Natural History, New York.
- **#43 Carmanah Giant:** the tallest measured Sitka spruce tree in the world, towers 95 m tall; approximately 400 years old. The entire Carmanah Valley, on the island's west coast, is protected as a provincial park.
- **#49 MV _Lady Rose_:** a heritage Coaster, last of the Union Steamship line, built in the late 1930s and still serving the Alberni Inlet and Barkley Sound, carrying cargo, mail and passengers.

Source: Encyclopedia of British Columbia.

HEALTH CARE

Number of physicians by census metropolitan area or census agglomeration, 2007:

	gp's/family doctors	specialists	total
Victoria	567	477	1,044
Nanaimo	121	104	225
Courtenay	88	49	137

Higher Education

University of Victoria (Victoria)
Public, degree-granting; established 1963.
Programs: Undergraduate and graduate programs in 10 faculties and 2 divisions.
Student enrollment: 19,500

Royal Roads University (Colwood)
Public, degree-granting; established 1995.
Programs: Undergraduate and graduate programs; certificate and diploma programs.
Student enrollment: 4,400

Vancouver Island University (Nanaimo)
Public, degree-granting; established 1969.
Programs: Graduate and undergraduate degrees, diplomas and certificates; English Language program.
Student enrollment: 11,000

Camosun College (Victoria)
Public; established 1971.
Programs: Credit, vocational, and continuing education programs.
Student enrollment: 15,400

North Island College (Campbell River, Comox Valley, Port Alberni, Port Hardy)
Public; established 1975.
Programs: Associate and Baccalaureate degrees.
Student enrollment: 3,700

Duncan	61	39	100
Campbell River	54	24	78
Parksville	34	10	44
Port Alberni	25	12	37

Source: CMA.

Weblinks

BC Statistics

www.bcstats.gov.bc.ca

They crunch the numbers. Vast arrays of statistics, many pertinent to Vancouver Island, many free.

VancouverIsland.com

www.vancouverisland.com

The first stop when you need information on Vancouver Island; everything from local town maps to job searches to the best places to eat.

Tourism Vancouver Island

www.vancouverisland.travel

Guides for visitors that are user-friendly for residents as well.

Take 5 VANCOUVER ISLAND'S FASTEST GROWING MUNICIPALITIES

Population in 2007 (with percentage growth over 2006)
1. **Langford 24,817** (+5.8)
2. **Courtenay 23,911** (+4.4)
3. **Cumberland 3,018** (+4.1)
4. **Ladysmith 8,144** (+3.3)
5. **Sooke 10,504** (+3.3)

Source: BC Statistics.

Slang

Few words and phrases are of genuine Vancouver Island origin. Many expressions in the following list have their origins elsewhere but are in common use on the islands, or once were. Language is always changing, and it's interesting to note that, in the early days of settlement the common language of commerce was a coastal patois called Chinook Jargon. Like so many local usages, Chinook became lost in the babble of the Global Village.

A-frame: A rig with long cables attached to a donkey engine, often on a raft floating in the chuck, operated by an independent logger, to yard logs down slopes; a common shoreline sight in the steam era; also, a common house design — for example, of chalets at Mt. Washington.

Alberni toothpick: A big log; old-time logger talk.

All Red Line: Global telegraph cable linking points in the British Empire (so named because maps of the day showed the Empire in red); the longest segment was 5,697 km between the Bamfield Cable Station on the west coast of Vancouver Island and Fanning Island. The Bamfield station operated from 1902 to 1959 with a large staff; now the site of the Bamfield Marine Sciences Centre.

Bathtub Race: A summertime melée of motorized vessels made of (or resembling) bathtubs and began in Nanaimo in 1967; in its heyday the course was from Nanaimo Harbour to Kitsilano Beach, Vancouver; it now involves a circuit of Winchelsea Island.

Banana Belt: Southeastern Vancouver Island and the Gulf Islands. It is Canada's mildest climate and is the place where the palm tree and cactus grow.

Beehive burner: These conspicuous conical consumers of sawmill waste (often with clouds of sparks above barely-screened domes) were once landmarks in many communities.

Black Ball Line: Puget Sound Navigation Co. services between Washington, USA and Vancouver Island, on such vessels as *Kalakala*, *Chinook* and *Kahloke*; the successor company was bought by the BC Government in 1958. Today Black Ball Transport Inc. (a distinct company) operates MV *Coho* between Port Angeles, WA and Victoria.

Blackdamp: Asphyxiating mix of carbon dioxide and water vapour exuded by coal into the tunnels of poorly-ventilated mines like those of the Dunsmuirs and other early industrialists on Vancouver Island (the symptoms of oxygen deprivation is indistinguishable from fatigue). More than 1,000 coal miners died on the job on Vancouver Island. Blackdamp was a silent killer.

Bongo brush: Forest-worker talk for the thick vegetation that takes over plantations, especially on the best growing sites, requiring quantities of herbicides to control.

Caddy or *Cadborosaurus*: A sea-monster named for Cadboro Bay, near Victoria, where it has often been sighted. It has only once been photographed since the 30s, although hundreds of sightings up and down the coast add to centuries-old legends about this apparent survivor from the age of dinosaurs. It is roughly 15 m long and sinuous, with a head like a horse or camel without the ears. Caddy has small anterior flippers but no posterior flippers, but has a large tailfin. In brief appearances, it shows one or more humps or coils and observers have noted that it is capable of swimming around 40 km per hour.

Caulks: Pronounced 'corks,' high-lacing logging boots with studded soles for traction on wet logs.

Chinook: Trading jargon or creole that evolved between First Nations and immigrant entrepreneurs as early as the 18th century. The pidgin pie of indigenous French and English words became widely used on the Pacific slope and was recorded in many phrase books. Originally Chinook was the name of an Oregon First Nation; in Canada, the name of a species of salmon (see tyee).

Chuck: Chinook jargon term for salt water.

CIL spinner: Old-time fishing at the Canadian Industries Ltd. explosives plant on James Island; light a stick of dynamite and throw it in the chuck, then scoop up the dead and unconscious fish.

The Colwood Crawl: Rush-hour bottleneck on Route 1 west of Victoria.

The Company: The Hudson's Bay Company, which established Fort Victoria (1843) and the Colony of Vancouver Island (1849) and pretty much ran things until after union with British Columbia and Canada. The company still operates a chain of department stores known as The Bay, three of which remain on the island.

CPR: 1. The Canadian Pacific Railway Company, which invested heavily in Vancouver Island, building the Coast Steamship Service of "Princess Ships" and the Empress Hotel. They also bought the Esquimalt and Nanaimo Railway, including the railway lands, which accounted for almost a quarter of the island's total land. It was a purchase historian W. Kaye Lamb called the best deal the company ever made.
2. Creeping Paralysis Railway, nickname for the Victoria & Sidney Railway (1892-1919), a 26 km wood-burning line with a flexible schedule and the habit of stopping in fields to load cordwood.

Donkey engine: Steam-powered winch, often mounted on sleds, for yarding (pulling logs to a landing).

Fixed Link: An often-discussed but unbuildable bridge or tunnel linking Vancouver Island and the mainland.

Follow the Birds to Victoria: Flocks of seagulls used to trail passenger vessels, which inspired this tourist slogan; the once-common practice of dumping food waste overboard persisted until the 80s.

Forestry: Forest industries generally, including logging and milling. Properly speaking, forestry is the art and science of growing trees.

Fulford dancing slippers: Gumboots.

The Galloping Goose: Multiple-use trail of converted railway right-of-way near Victoria. The original Goose was a gas-powered dayliner that ran between Victoria and Youbou in the 20s.

The Goat Ranch: Old-time brothel near Port Alberni.

Graveyard of the Pacific: The stretch of west coast Vancouver Island opposite the entrance to the Strait of Juan de Fuca where dozens of ships were driven on-shore in heavy seas.

Gulf of Georgia: Misnomer for the Strait of Georgia that originated in Capt. George Vancouver's initial impression (1792) that Vancouver Island was really just part of the mainland, and the body of water had only one outlet, which was at the south; hence the Gulf Islands. The name of the body of water was corrected by Capt. Richards in 1865, but the old usage persists.

Take 5 TOM PARKIN'S
ISLAND WAYS WITH WORDS

Tom Parkin, author of *Wet Coast Words* (Orca, 1989), compiled his dictionary of BC words and phrases with a lot of public participation, often appearing on talk shows soliciting submissions. Parkin, formerly a writer by profession, is now a Nanaimo stonemason. He has lived on Vancouver Island since 1987.

1. **Boneyize** was contributed by a Vancouver resident and recently heard at Youbou, Vancouver Island. It's a kid's expression from the 40s that means "first dibs" — "I boneyize that."

2. **The Big Island:** The Gulf Islands each have their own character, and Vancouver Island is the Big Island, as Hawaii is the Big Island in that archipelago.

3. **Kiss-me-arse:** The Marbled Murrelet, a west coast seabird that nests in old-growth forests, characteristically swims ahead of approaching boats and impudently flips its tail as it dives to safety.

4. **Mowitch:** A Chinook term meaning deer or venison. I've often heard it used on Vancouver Island.

5. Islanders sometimes pronounce words in a peculiar way — "shalal" instead of "salal," "Kok-i-silah" for "Koksilah;" "Mala-sa-pina" instead of "Malaspina." These misspeakings are so commonplace as to be elements of a regional dialect.

Harvesting: Logging; properly speaking the term, from crop agriculture, pertains to planted and tended second-growth forests. It is unfortunately also applied indiscriminately to Old Growth forests, a non-replaceable resource; the extraction of which is more accurately likened to mining.

The Hump: The long hill up and out of Port Alberni eastbound on Route 4 and the down-slope to the Cameron River.

Take 5 DAVID ROBERTSON'S CHARACTERISTICS OF VANCOUVER ISLAND DIALECT

David Robertson has made a special study of Chinook Jargon in his capacity as a linguist working on his Ph.D. at the University of Victoria.

1. Mainstream Vancouver Island English isn't so divergent from that of the Lower Mainland, and both have become such crossroads that you find a bit of a blend of all Canadian varieties, much as has happened in the formation of a general western USA dialect.

2. The two regions definitely share a few Chinook Jargon loans that are still in casual use. I have heard plenty of "skookum" (attributive/predicative adjective). Most Chinook Jargon terms, however, have dropped out of use among the younger generations, who don't usually recognize "siwash," "cultus," and "the chuck."

3. Lots of localisms like "People's Republic of Fernwood," "The Malahat," "up-island," or "Sooke" as a bastion of free spirits or "Nanaimo" as the epitome of a working-class town...

4. Native communities most definitely have their localisms in English. They'll often be found in other places. An example is "a burning," a particular post-death ceremony among the Coast Salish of Vancouver Island. And "big house," and derivatives like "big-house speaker."

5. As is true of Canadian English as a whole, Vancouver Island's regional dialect is distinguished most clearly by the combination of features it contains. No other place has the particular grouping of influences.

Killer Whale: Orca, a toothed black-and-white whale (*Orcinus orca*) with a prominent dorsal fin, weighing up to 8 tonnes. It is common in the waters around Vancouver Island. For many years they were known as blackfish and shot by fishers or, beginning in the 1960s, captured and penned in aquaria. They are well-studied in the wild, particularly by John Ford, Graeme Ellis, Paul Spong, et al.; several resident populations inhabit protected inside waters, while transient populations have much larger ranges; pods (large family groups) are matriarchal.

Klee Wyck (*Nuu-Chah-Nulth*, *"laughing one"*): The nickname given to Emily Carr when she visited Ucluelet in 1899, as told in the first chapter of her first book, *Klee Wyck*, published 1941.

Log boom: Long rafts of logs towed by tugs to mills, once a common sight along the coast of Vancouver Island. There were literally booms in every bay and cove. Booms often broke up in storms on the west coast and the Strait of Juan de Fuca and the loss of fibre from towing mishaps was astronomical.

Lotus Land: The good life on Vancouver Island, epitomized by Bruce Hutchison in *The Unknown Country* (1941). He borrowed a phrase often used to describe California, from Homer's *The Odyssey*, where Odysseus describes a narrow escape from the island of "the Lotus-eaters, who had no thought of killing my comrades, but gave them lotus to eat. Those who ate the honey-sweet lotus fruit no longer wished to bring back word to us, or sail for home. They wanted to stay with the Lotus-eaters, eating the lotus, forgetting all thoughts of return."

Maggie: Nickname for TEV *Princess Marguerite II*, a CPR pocket cruiser that plied the protected waters between Victoria, Vancouver and Seattle from 1949-1988. A predecessor of the same name was in service from 1925 to 1942.

The Malahat: Scenic Malahat Drive is a section of Route 1 near Victoria, surmounting a ridge on the west side of Saanich Inlet; named for the Malahat First Nation.

Mile Zero: Pacific terminus of the Trans-Canada Highway. It is at the foot of Douglas Street, Victoria.

More English than the English: Emily Carr's description of her father — applicable to early Victoria.

Nanaimo bar: A layered, chilled confection of cracker crumbs, coconut, chocolate, sugar and butter. It is of uncertain origin — possibly the *Vancouver Sun*, possibly the 1952 *Women's Auxiliary to the Nanaimo Hospital Cook Book*.

Pat Bay: Patricia Bay, north of Victoria; also the name of the airstrip established there in the 1930s as an RAF training centre (now Victoria International Airport). It is also the name of Route 17, the highway to the airport and BC Ferries' Swartz Bay terminal (the Pat Bay Highway does not, however, go to Pat Bay).

Pusser's Corner: A bus stop at the corner of Yates and Douglas streets in Victoria, where sailors returning to the Esquimalt naval base gathered. The name is slang for "purser" (a ship's supply officer) and in British naval parlance meant "one hundred percent Service."

Did you know...

that the *Dictionary of Canadianisms on Historical Principles*, the only standard work of its kind in Canada, was prepared by the Lexicographical Centre for Canadian English at the University of Victoria and published by W.J. Gage Ltd in 1967? Matthew Harry Scargill was director of the centre as well as the founding head (and only professor) of the fledgling university's department of linguistics, the first in English-speaking Canada. A native of Yorkshire, Prof. Scargill was the driving force behind the project. It has not yet been revised.

Raging Grannies: Colourful anti-war protest group formed in Victoria in 1987, singing songs off-key in public places; unaffiliated groups soon formed in other cities.

Rainshadow: a region on the lee side of mountains that receives less rainfall than the region on the windward side.

Remittance man: A British younger son who migrated to the frontier to farm or log and whose family supported him by remitting a regular stipend.

The Sommers Affair: Notorious corruption case surrounding the award of exclusive tree-cutting rights to E.P. Taylor's BC Forest Products Ltd. in 1953. Minister of Forests Robert Sommers, a former elementary school principal, was found to have taken bribes, including rugs valued at $607 in his Victoria home, and served time. It was the first such conviction of an elected official serving as minister in any government in the British Commonwealth.

Stand: A forest, commercially considered.

The Tweed Curtain: Border of Oak Bay, mythic land of white ducks, cricket, a squeeze of lemon in your Earl Grey.

Tyee (*Chinook Jargon*): Chief; thus *Hyas Kloochman Tyee* = great + woman + chief = Queen Victoria. It is also a large Chinook salmon, in the parlance of Campbell River.

Up-Island: North of Victoria.

Wobblies: The International Workers of the World (IWW), founded in Chicago in 1905. It was less influential on Vancouver Island than the United Mine Workers of America (UMWA), which funded and sustained the Big Strike of 1912-14; or the International Woodworkers of America (IWA), which organized the forests in the 30s.

Wrangellia: The original Vancouver Island, a terrane that cozied up to the North American main some 100 million years ago.

Place Names

Vancouver Island's unique history is spelled out in its cities and towns, its bays and inlets and its lofty mountain peaks, where names of Spanish ancestry practically rub letters with those of First Nations and British heritage on maps of the Island.

While some names baffle newcomers — 'how do you pronounce Ucluelet?' — all are poetic reminders of the people who came before us and hint at stories that might otherwise be forgotten. Just think, if Captain James Vancouver or Captain Juan Francisco de la Bodega y Quadra could return to Vancouver Island today, they would still recognize many places by name... names that they and other early explorers chose and put on the first maps.

Alert Bay: This small community of 550 people on tiny Cormorant Island, off the east coast of Vancouver Island, was named after the *HM Alert*, the first steam powered vessel to visit, in 1860.

Barkley Sound: Captain Charles William Barkley named this large inlet on the west coast of the island in 1787 when he visited the area onboard the *Imperial Eagle*.

Buttle Lake: This large lake in Strathcona Provincial Park was named after Commander John Buttle, a geologist and botanist from Kew Gardens in London, who explored the central part of the Island in 1864-1865.

Cathedral Grove: Some of the trees in this ancient forest were already old when Captain Cook set foot on Vancouver Island in 1778. The name was well-established as far back as 1921. Since 1947, some 136 ha. of the forest have been protected in H. R. MacMillan Provincial Park, the gift of the timber tycoon. Perhaps early visitors found the towering trees as inspirational as a cathedral.

Campbell River: The largest city on the north island took the name of the river flowing through it, which was named by Captain Richards for Samuel Campbell, a surgeon aboard the HMS *Plumper* from 1857 to 1861.

Chemainus: The east coast town known for its colourful outdoor murals has an equally interesting story behind its name. In the Halkomelem language, 'Tsa-mee-mis' means 'bitten breast' and apparently refers to the horseshoe shape of the bay, which appears to have a bite taken out of it.

Coombs: The Salvation Army brought impoverished English and Welsh settlers here at the turn of the 20th century and named the community after the Army's Canadian Commissioner, Captain Thomas Coombs.

Cortes Island: Spanish naval officers named this island between Campbell River and the mainland in 1792 in honour of Hernando Cortes, the conqueror of Mexico.

Did you know...

that there are only three other bodies of water in the world that are similar to Saanich Inlet, with shallow sills at the mouths? Saanich Inlet's mouth is 75 m deep but towards the head of the inlet, the depth plunges to 230 m.

Have A Little R-E-S-P-E-C-T

Nanaimo is the best-located city on Vancouver Island, with a diverse economy and the cultural life of a centre much larger than its 100,000 people. The Hub City is equally convenient to the mountain wilds and the west coast as it is to Georgia Strait and Vancouver. No wonder it has become ultra desirable as a place to live and work, with a full-fledged university and a growing high-tech community. Nanaimo has long since lived down its black, black past — so why can't it get any respect?

The city's very existence stemmed from the discovery of coal in 1849. Originally a Hudson's Bay Company operation like Victoria, Nanaimo was named for the Snuneymuxw First Nation. Bearing witness to long possession of the area by this Coast Salish people are shell middens, burial sites, petroglyphs and culturally modified trees. It was actually First Nations people who discovered the coal and alerted the HBC.

Coal mines were Nanaimo's staple industry for nearly a century, when thousands of workers and their families lived by the whistle. By 1950 all the big mines but No.10 at South Wellington had closed — leaving, TW Paterson wrote in *Ghost Town Trails on Vancouver Island*, "a collection of abandoned and flooded workings, weed-choked railway tracks which led to nowhere and dozens of dilapidated buildings" — this in the middle of town. Some wrote the city off, predicting that grass would soon grow in the streets.

Construction of the Harmac pulp mill south of town in 1950 helped Nanaimo to reinvent itself. (The name Harmac is a contraction of Harvey MacMillan — it was the industrialist's cable name.) Since the mill recently closed — probably forever — along with the Harmac sawmill, the curtain has fallen on that era, too.

Today, the retail trade is a major part of Nanaimo's economy, employing 15 percent of the workforce, as the city continues to function as a supply centre for much of the island. Nanaimo is believed to have the most retail space per capita of any city in North America. Its many shopping malls do a huge trade with surrounding communities.

They Said It

> "Señor Quadra has very earnestly requested that I would name some port or island after us both, to commemorate our meeting and the very friendly intercourse that had taken place and subsisted between us. Conceiving no spot so proper for this denomination as the place where we had first met, which was nearly in the centre of a tract of land that had first been circumnavigated by us... I named that country the island of QUADRA and VANCOUVER; with which compliment he seemed highly pleased."
>
> **– Captain George Vancouver, 1792**

Clayoquot Sound: This area of indented coastline on the west coast was named for the aboriginal people living there. 'Tla-o' or 'Cla-o' means 'different' or 'another' and 'aht' means 'village' or 'people' in the local language. According to one source, the Clayoquot people were once quiet and peaceful but became quarrelsome later on. Perhaps the name foretold that Clayoquot Sound would one day be the site of the largest peaceful protest in Canada.

Comox: The east coast town which is home to Canadian Forces Base Comox was originally home to the Puntledge and Sloslute people, who called the area Komuckway or Comuckthway, which translates to 'plenty', 'abundance' or 'riches' and probably referred to the plentiful game and berries.

Courtenay: The major centre in the Comox Valley got its name from the adjacent river, which in turn was named for Captain George William Conway Courtenay of the HMS *Constance* in the mid-1800s.

Desolation Sound: When he explored here and named the area in 1792, Captain Vancouver didn't find anything uplifting in what is now a hugely popular boating and kayaking destination.

The Jewel in the Crown

Queen Victoria was 24 years old when, in 1843, some of her subjects in the Hudson's Bay Company hired the indigenous Lekwungen Coast Salish people on distant Vancouver Island to put up a fort, and they named it Fort Victoria in her honour. With the provincial government and a navy base as its anchors, Victoria had a second career as a regional centre of industry, trade and shipbuilding. The smokestacks are long gone, but the Old Lady has done okay anyway. Today, a city of 350,000 smug souls gives the lie to the old clichés.

One hoary cliché is "a little bit of old England." Do Victorians really inhabit some retro-world of doilies and jodhpurs? What about all those London double-decker buses? It's true that the tourist industry trafficks in Victoria's British heritage, with double-decker bus tours, crumpets and tea, and all that — and everyone appreciates that it would be a smaller, poorer place without the ±3.5 million visitors Victoria attracts every year. But nearly a quarter of the Victoria Regional Transit fleet of 238 buses are also double-deckers — efficient, contemporary working buses, integral to the transit system. Besides, Victoria pitches a different theme to tourists now — about being in the natural world — while in their civic sensibility, Victorians are linked with Los Angeles and Beijing no less than with London.

How about this one: Victoria as the resort of "the newly wed and the nearly dead"? Does, in other words, the city make a living from tourists, whether honeymooning or not, and home-buying retirees? Both are true, but only to a degree. It's true that the southeastern island and the Gulf Islands have huge proportions of seniors age 70 and over. It's true there is a sizeable retirement industry that provides a whole galaxy of goods and services to seniors. But the red-hot housing market, with some of the highest prices in Canada in the winter of 2008, is fuelled by younger, in-migrating home-buyers, including the first wave of retiring Baby Boomers and many big-city refugees. As for economic diversity, Victoria is successfully established as a high-tech centre, even as it finds new tourist niche markets to exploit.

It comes down to location — simply one of the most magnificent settings in the world, and the marvels of nature on every side. Victorians appreciate that — and they also bank on it.

Esperanza Inlet: Captain Cook originally called the inlet between Nootka Sound and Kyuquot Sound on the west coast 'Hope Bay'. It was later translated into the Spanish equivalent by Alexandro Malaspina, an Italian aristocrat in the Spanish navy. Malaspina is associated with the Nanaimo area but he never actually explored the east coast of the island.

Esquimalt: The Coast Salish people who lived here called it 'Is-whoy-malth', which means 'the place of gradually shoaling water'. True to its name, Esquimalt has tidal flats at the head of the harbour.

Gabriola Island: Just off Nanaimo, Gabriola was almost certainly named by a Spaniard, but which one, and why, is still being debated. It's possible that Jose Maria Narvaez called the east end of the island Gaviola, a name of Spanish aristocrats, or that Juan Francisco Bodega y Quadra named the island in honour of Simón de Gaviola y Zabala, paymaster of a Spanish fleet.

Galiano Island: Spanish commander Dionisio Alcala Galiano lent his name to this long narrow Gulf Island in 1859, having explored the area in 1792. Galiano was killed fighting the British in the Battle of Trafalgar.

Gold River: Spaniards searching for gold in the 1780s called this spot Rio del Oro, or River of Gold. A planned community established in the 1960s to house forest industry workers' families was the first in Canada to have underground wiring.

Did you know...

that Qualicum Beach is home to the most complete Ice Age walrus ever found on North America's west coast? 'Rambling Rosie' is estimated to be 70,000 years old, and is showcased at the Qualicum Beach Historical and Museum Society.

Golden Hinde: Originally called Rooster's Comb, the highest mountain on Vancouver Island was renamed in 1939 to commemorate the voyage of Sir Francis Drake in his flagship, the *Golden Hinde*. Drake may have sailed in these latitudes in 1579 while looking for the Northwest Passage. The renaming marked his 360th anniversary and the 360 degrees of the globe.

Take 5 KEVIN SMITH'S GREAT
PLACES TO VISIT

Kevin Smith is the owner of eco-tourism company Maple Leaf Adventures and captain of the schooner *Maple Leaf*, BC's heritage tall ship. A former backcountry park ranger on Vancouver Island, he was born and raised on Salt Spring Island and Vancouver Island. The *Maple Leaf* takes people to see the best wilderness areas on the BC coast.

1. **Brooks Peninsula:** This wild corner of Vancouver Island is so far west it's thought to have escaped glaciation in the last ice age and become a refuge for many plants and animals. This roadless wilderness with long sandy beaches is home to rafts of sea otters, nesting puffins, sea lions, albatrosses, and more. Only those with an adventurous spirit have seen it — and that keeps it special.
2. **Victoria's Inner Harbour:** History layers itself thickly in this beautiful natural harbour. Several places were Lekwungen village sites. Fort Victoria was situated here in 1843, and ships from across the Commonwealth traded here during Victoria's economic leadership of the early 1900s. It is still a working harbour, the seat of government, and a beautiful place to see.
3. **Blackney Pass:** Possibly the best place on the planet to view orcas. Resident family groups transit back and forth at this natural crossroads every day each summer and fall.
4. **Cape Sutil:** The true northern tip of Vancouver Island.
5. **Cowichan, Comox and Saanich:** Three warm, fertile areas where Vancouver Island's local food is grown.

They Said It

Hornby Island: This popular summer holiday destination was named after Phipps Hornby, Commander-in-Chief of Britain's Pacific fleet from 1847 to 1851.

Kadonaga Bay: This name was adopted in 2007 in recognition of the first Japanese settler to Mayne Island, Gontaro (Goan) Kadonaga, and in honour of all Japanese settlers who contributed to the island before being removed during World War II. Kadonaga arrived in 1903 after purchasing 160 acres on the eastern tip of the island. Approximately one-third of Mayne Island's population were of Japanese descent prior to the war.

Kyuquot: Pronounced 'Ky-YOU-cut', the name of this mainly Aboriginal community means 'land of many winds', a fitting description for its windswept location on the northwest end of Vancouver Island.

Ladysmith: Originally known as Oyster Harbour, coal baron James Dunsmuir changed the town's name in 1900 upon hearing that the British had relieved the siege of Ladysmith in South Africa. He went on to name streets in Ladysmith after heroes from the Boer war.

Lasqueti Island: Named in 1791 for Spanish naval officer Juan Maria Lasqueti, the island was home to Aboriginal people when Europeans first arrived, and is now home to about 350 equally self-reliant folk, who don't mind the lack of electricity and paved roads.

Malahat: The mountainous overpass on the west side of Saanich Inlet could mean 'place of bait' or could refer to a caterpillar infestation, depending which First Nation you ask. 'Place of accidents' may be the best definition these days, given the number of automobile crashes here each year.

Mayne Island: British navy captain George Richards named this Gulf Island for his lieutenant, Richard Charles Mayne.

Mitlenatch Island: This rocky island between Campbell River and the mainland is a provincial park and has the largest seabird colony in the Strait of Georgia. In the Coast Salish language, its name means 'calm waters all around.'

Mount Cain: This mountain and nearby Mount Abel on northern Vancouver Island were named after the infamous brothers from the Old Testament. Mount Eden is adjacent, which only seems appropriate, given that the brothers' parents were Adam and Eve.

Mount Tzouhalem: The mountain above Cowichan Bay is where Aboriginal warrior Tzouhalem is said to have lived in a cave after being driven out of his own village. As well as treating his own people brutally, he terrified white settlers in the mid-1800s, at one point attacking Fort Victoria.

Nanaimo: Vancouver Island's second largest city refers to the Coast Salish people who wintered here. Different spellings and interpretations include 'Sne-ny-mo' — 'a big strong tribe' and 'Sna Ney Mous' — 'meeting place'.

Nootka Island: When Captain Cook arrived here in 1778, the native people apparently yelled out, "itchme nutka, itchme nutka" which means 'go around', but Cook and his crew thought they were giving the name of their island.

> *"The place itself appears a perfect Eden in the midst of the dreary wilderness of the Northwest coast, and so different in its general aspect, from the wooded rugged regions around, that one might be pardoned for supposing it had dropped from the clouds into its present position."*
>
> **– James Douglas, in a letter describing his first landing near Clover Point, Victoria, in 1842.**

Port Alberni: The city took its name from the Alberni Canal, which was named in 1791 for Dom Pedro Alberni. The Spanish commander was part of an expedition sent by the Viceroy of Mexico to occupy the west coast and enforce Spanish sovereignty.

Port McNeill: This town on the northeast coast of Vancouver Island was named for William Henry McNeill, captain of the Hudson's Bay Company ship, the *SS Beaver*, the first steamship to visit the coast.

Quadra Island: Home of Kwakwak'awakw First Nation members and about 3,000 more recent arrivals, Quadra Island was named for Spanish naval officer Juan Francisco de la Bodega y Quadra.

Salt Spring Island: The name was inspired by 14 briny springs on the island and recorded as early as 1855 in a Hudson's Bay Company map. A few years later Captain Richards tried to rename it Admiral Island, but locals continued to call it Salt Spring Island, a name officially adopted by the Geographic Board of Canada in 1910.

Saturna Island: Renowned for its annual Canada Day lamb barbeque, Saturna Island was named after the Spanish naval schooner *Saturnina* in 1791.

Sooke: The name of this rainforest town came from the local Salish First Nation, the T'sou-ke, who apparently took their name from the stickleback fish they caught in the mouth of the river.

Sointula: This small island across from Port McNeill means 'place of harmony' in Finnish, the language of its original settlers, who moved here in 1901 to establish a socialist commune.

Strathcona Park: British Columbia's oldest provincial park was named after Donald Alexander Smith, a Scottish immigrant, Hudson's Bay Company trader, provincial and federal politician, and a director and financier of the Canadian Pacific Railway. In 1897, in honour of his contribution to the development of Canada, he was elevated to the peerage, with the title Baron Strathcona and Mount Royal.

Tofino: This popular tourist town close to Pacific Rim National Park takes its name from nearby Tofino Inlet, which was named in 1792 by Spanish commanders Galiano and Valdes in honour of Don Vicente Tofiño, a rear admiral in the Spanish navy.

Ucluelet: As any boater on the west coast knows, Ucluelet offers a sheltered harbour from wild weather. The local Aboriginal people were called 'Yu-clutl-ahts' which means 'the people with the safe landing place'.

Victoria: The largest city on Vancouver Island and BC's capital, Victoria was named in 1843 for the reigning monarch, Queen Victoria.

Wickanninish Beach: This west coast beach recalls chief of the Tla-o-qui-aht First Nation during the late 18th century, when Europeans first made contact. Captain Meares reportedly traded two copper kettles for about 50 sea otter pelts from Chief Wickanninish.

Yuquot: Translated as Friendly Cove, this community of Mowachaht people on the southern tip of Nootka Island is steeped in aboriginal and colonial history. It was here that Captain Cook came ashore.

Zeballos: This 1930s-era gold-rush village is at the end of a gravel-logging road on Zeballos Inlet. The inlet was named by Captain Malaspina in 1791 for Lieutenant Ciriaco Cevallos, an officer in his expedition. (Zeballos is another spelling of Cevallos.)

Natural World

Vancouver Island is no longer, as artist Emily Carr put it, "the edge of nowhere." What has put the island on the map is nature. It is a land of natural wonders and superlatives, diverse and rugged enough to retain intact wilderness even after a hundred years of serious timber extraction. The celebrated west coast lifestyle is based largely on access to environment. As its population and fame increase so do the pressures on the land.

GEOLOGIC ORIGINS

Vancouver Island actually originated close to the Equator where, 380 million years ago, the oldest rocks were formed by undersea lava flows. Almost as old are the limestones formed of seashell sediments. Succeeding ages added much volcanism, and sedimentation.

These rocks were part of Wrangellia Terrane, which migrated into position against the North American plate about 100 million years ago. Two smaller terranes, the Pacific Rim and the Crescent, were in place by 42 million years before present. Uplift, volcanism, faulting, folding, sedimentation, granitic intrusion and other forces created many of the landscapes of Vancouver Island.

Episodes of glaciation added vast deposits of till, most recently less than 15,000 years ago. On the west coast the glaciers carved deep inlets and created huge beaches. They exposed and scoured surface rock across the southeast coast and in the Gulf Islands.

Sources: The Geology of Southern Vancouver Island and "The Geology and Geological History of Vancouver Island."

LATITUDE AND LONGITUDE

Vancouver Island's southernmost reach is Christopher Point (latitude 48°18'N), and its northernmost shore is near Jepther Point (50°52'34"N). Its westernmost limit is near Cape Scott, at longitude 128°25'52"W, while the most easterly spot is near Cadboro Point (123°15'51"W).

Victoria, the largest city, is on the same latitude as Munich, Germany and Paris, France, and the same longitude as Seattle, Washington and San Francisco, California.

Size: 31,285 km^2

GREATER VANCOUVER ISLAND

Some numbers in this chapter give Vancouver Island's total area as 33,650 km^2, which includes all islands on the west side of Vancouver Island and, on the east side, the Gulf Islands, Lasqueti, Denman, Hornby, Quadra, Cortes, Malcolm and Cormorant islands.

Source: BC Statistics.

Emily Carr

Emily Carr (1871-1945) is towering figure in Vancouver Island history. The reverence with which she is held permeates island life today and her ideas and thoughts reflect an emerging island identity. She was an extraordinary artist of nature who brought the west coast to the world's attention. She was born in Victoria and studied art in San Francisco, London and Paris. Unmarried and in her 40s, and discouraged by economic hardship and lack of success, she returned to Victoria and gave up painting to run a rooming house a stone's throw from her birthplace.

Years later, her paintings of First Nations villages would catch the eye of anthropologist Marius Barbeau and Group of Seven artist Lawren Harris. Their appreciation kindled the renewal of her work as an artist. In Carr's later expressionist oil paintings, she takes the viewer inside Vancouver Island's ancient temperate rainforest.

She painted clearcuts near Shawnigan Lake. In one painting, the glowing firmament is broken by a single towering Douglas fir (Scorned as Timber, Beloved of the Sky, 1935). Carr brought the same nature-centred spirituality to her paintings of First Nations village ruins (Forsaken, 1937). When she suffered a heart attack and could no longer roam, she took up writing and published three collections of vivid stories about her life. (Others were published posthumously.)

Carr has now become a Canadian icon, and her star is still rising. Paintings that Carr might have sold for a few dollars have recently fetched more than a million. She now keeps company with Frida Kahlo (Mexico) and Georgia O'Keeffe (USA). A *New York Times* review of the 2002 exhibit "Carr, O'Keeffe, Kahlo: Places of Their Own," quotes curator Sharyn Udall as saying that these three great artists "were redefining a landscape aesthetic in their own terms and through the eyes of women." Few of Emily Carr's masterworks remained in Victoria.

Take 5 VANCOUVER ISLAND'S
FIVE HIGHEST POINTS

1. **Golden Hinde** 2,220 m
2. **Elkhorn Mountain** 2,166 m
3. **Victoria Peak** 2,163 m
4. **Mount Colonel Foster** 2,135 m
5. **Rambler Peak** 2,105 m

Source: Beyond Nootka: A Historical Perspective of Vancouver Island Mountains.

VANCOUVER ISLAND . . .

- Is the largest island on the west coast of the Americas.
- Is the 11th largest island in Canada — bigger than Somerset Island (24,786 km^2), but smaller than Prince of Wales (33,339 km^2).
- Is the 42nd largest island in the world — bigger than Timor (30,777 km^2), smaller than Hainan (33,572 km^2), and more than 1/3 the size of Great Britain (83,698 km^2).
- Is nearly 6 times larger than Prince Edward Island (5,660 km^2).
- Occupies 3.3 percent of British Columbia's total area, and 0.3 percent of Canada's.

Sources: World Island Information and Atlas of Canada.

Did you know...

that thousands of kilometres of logging roads lace the island? If on Crown land, they are open to the public. Active logging roads require visitors to yield right-of-way to trucks. Local knowledge is often required.

Did you know...

the record for a solo kayak circumnavigation of Vancouver Island — a straight-line distance of about 1,200 km — is 24 days, by Joe O'Blenis, who completed the trip in the summer of 2007?

Take 5 VANCOUVER ISLAND'S
FIVE LARGEST RIVERS

WATERSHED AREA (km²)

1. **Nimpkish**	1,760
2. **Somass**	1,280
3. **Campbell**	1,470
4. **Gold**	992
5. **Salmon**	1,200

Sources: Water Survey of Canada and Environment Canada.

AS THE CROW FLIES

- Length: 454 km (Cape Scott to Cadboro Point)
- Widest width: 132 km (Chatham Point to Estevan Point)
- Narrowest width: 24 km (Qualicum Bay to Alberni Inlet)
- Average width: 81 km (Qualicum Bay to Cape Beale)

Length of coastline: 3,226 km

BOUNDARIES

- West: Pacific Ocean, Strait of Juan de Fuca
- Southeast: Haro Strait, Strait of Georgia
- Northeast: Discovery Passage, Johnstone Strait, Broughton Strait, Queen Charlotte Strait, Goletas Channel
- North: Queen Charlotte Sound

Did you know...

that the Douglas fir is not a true fir but a 'false hemlock' (*Pseudotsuga*)? It was named after Scottish botanist David Douglas, and it's been called everything from a spruce (Douglas, red or yellow) to Oregon pine to *sapin* [fir] *de Douglas*. The coastal variety ranges from Northern California (latitude 36°N) to northern BC (53°N).

DISTANCES FROM VICTORIA

Vancouver, BC	91 km
Nanaimo, BC	97 km
Seattle, USA	115 km
Los Angeles, USA	1,645 km
Ottawa, ON	3,585 km
Maui, USA	4,263 km
St. John's, NL	5,080 km

LIE OF THE LAND

The Vancouver Island Mountains extend almost the entire length of Vancouver Island. They rise up to 2,200 m above seal level, trending northwest in a line, in effect dividing the island in two.

The west side is wild, rugged and deeply indented. The open Pacific pounds the west coast, and winter storms lash its slopes. Geographers refer to this region as the Windward Island Mountains ecosection.

The east side is drier and somewhat less rugged. The Leeward Island Mountains ecosection is bounded on the north by Johnstone Strait, on the south by the Strait of Juan de Fuca, and on the southeast by a lowland plain.

The urbanized southeast coast is noticeably flatter, drier and gen-

Did you know...

that beautiful Garry oak meadows once spread throughout drier sites of southeastern Vancouver Island and the Gulf Islands — but are now drastically reduced? Ecologists have used historic records, even old photographs, to reconstruct their original extent. Before European settlement more than 120 km² of Garry oak ecosystems flourished in deep soil (there was less growing on rocky baulds). Urbanization has disturbed nearly 99 percent of the deep-soil ecosystems. Only 175 ha. remain undisturbed.

tler. Known as the Nanaimo Lowlands ecosection, its high scenic values and rainshadow climate give the island a Lotus Land character. Clustered along the lowlands and even drier is the Southern Gulf Islands ecosection.

On the northeast side, the mountains subside and the valleys broaden. There's a partial rainshadow in these Northern Island Mountains. The north end of Vancouver Island is a coastal plain known as the Nahwitti Lowland, where it's very wet.

Sources: BC Government and Dictionary.com.

Take 5 VANCOUVER ISLAND'S RECORD CONIFERS

	CIRCUMFERENCE (m)	HEIGHT (m)
Canada's largest tree: western red cedar, Cheewhat Lake	18.3	55.5
World's largest Douglas fir: Red Creek	13.3	73.8
Canada's tallest spruce: The Carmanah Giant, Sitka spruce	9.9	96.0
Canada's largest yellow cedar: Memekay River	10.4	46.9
Canada's largest Shore pine: Esquimalt	3.3	18.2

Source: Register of Big Trees in B.C.

GETTING AROUND

Highways:

- 1 - Victoria to Nanaimo (Trans-Canada Highway)
- 1A - North Cowichan to Ladysmith
- 4 - Qualicum Beach to Tofino
- 14 - Langford to Port Renfrew (West Coast Highway)
- 17 - Victoria to Swartz Bay (Patricia Bay Highway)
- 18 - North Cowichan to Lake Cowichan
- 19 - Duke Point to Bear Cove (Inland Island Highway)
- 19A - Nanaimo to Campbell River (Island Highway)
- 28 - Campbell River to Gold River
- 30 - from Route 19 north of Port McNeill to Port Alice

Source: BC Government.

THROUGH THE MOUNTAINS

The southern ranges can be reached via Route 18, through the Cowichan Valley. Many logging roads are on private land and gated. The most-travelled road to the West Coast is Route 4, via Port Alberni. The higher central ranges are accessible via Route 28 through Strathcona Provincial Park, west of Campbell River. A road through the northern ranges begins at Woss Camp, off Route 19 west of Sayward.

Take 5 BRIONY PENN'S
ENVIRONMENTAL BRIGHT LIGHTS

Briony Penn, Ph.D., is a naturalist, geographer and writer. Born in Victoria, she currently lives on Salt Spring Island.

1. **Eelgrass restoration**. Eelgrass meadows are an important feature of the intertidal zone in estuaries. They are critical habitat for young salmon, herring and other marine life. Nikki Wright started Seachange to educate, map and restore damaged eelgrass beds, reaching out to a wide range of community groups in the process.

2. **Native bee habitat restoration**. Rex Welland, a Saanich orchardist and master of heritage apple varieties, has stimulated a renaissance in protecting native bees and their habitat after years of watching declining pollination rates and declining health in the domesticated, imported honeybee populations.

3. **Restoration of traditional First Nations food**. Cheryl Bryce of the Songhees First Nation is spearheading the cultivation and harvesting of the lily camas, an important part of the endangered Garry oak ecosystem. Camas is valuable in the diet of First Nations people because it produces a different starch than the potato, which is associated with the high incidence of diabetes among the population. In restoring culture, she is restoring ecosystems, and vice versa.

4. **Slow food**. The idea of growing and consuming food locally came to Vancouver Island with Sinclair Philip, co-proprietor of Sooke Harbour House inn and restaurant, and chef Mara Jernigan, of Fairburn Farm in the Cowichan Valley. The slow food movement has become important to the economy of both these communities. Locally-trained author James MacKinnon co-wrote *The 100 Mile Diet*, which has caught on nationwide.

5. **The Land Conservancy of BC**. Established on Vancouver Island in 1997 to protect special places, and modeled on the National Trust of Britain, it has acquired and protected in some way thousands of hectares of properties, from heritage houses to entire watersheds. TLC has set up innovative models of land use that respect our natural and cultural heritage, from ranching and agricultural co-ops to recreational lands and sacred sites.

They Said It

"Why can't we secure parks and wilderness areas and wild rivers and the other spectacular things of the continent hard and fast in the heart of the Constitution, so that they will be safe from violation even if the biggest goddamned diamond mine or oil well or underground facsimile of the whole General Motors complex is found in one of them? Why not? Has industry some inalienable right to invade public lands wherever found and destroy them? ...
Ecologies must be recognized, assessed, understood, and defined; only then can they be adequately protected."

— **Roderick Haig-Brown in "Some Approaches to Conservation."**

THE COWICHAN RIVER

The Cowichan River follows a 47 km route through the verdant Cowichan Valley, flowing near the city of Duncan and the ancient villages of the Quw'utsun' (Cowichan) First Nation. The Cowichan River footpath makes accessible the 20 km of the river between Holt Creek and Skutz Falls, and the Trans-Canada Trail follows an old railroad right-of-way. Much of this recreation corridor is protected in the 14 km^2 Cowichan River Provincial Park. The estuary on Cowichan Bay is an outstanding wildlife area. In 2005, the Cowichan was included in the Canadian Heritage Rivers system.

Sources: Government of BC and the Canadian Heritage Rivers System.

Did you know...

that most dominant and codominant trees in old-growth forests on Vancouver Island are 200 to 350 years old? The median tree age was 270 years, with a slightly higher mean of 296 years.

Did you know...

that Vancouver Island is home to North America's most concentrated population of cougars?

LAND COVER

Of Vancouver Island's total area of 33,450 km^2 . . .

- 88.7 percent is forested
- 7.7 percent is alpine tundra, glaciers, estuaries, bog or swamp
- 2.7 percent is urban or industrial
- 0.9 percent is agricultural

Source: Vancouver Island Land Use Plan.

Take 5 CHRIS YORATH'S FAVORITE
PLACES TO LOOK AT ROCKS

Dr. Chris Yorath was a research geologist with the Geological Survey of Canada 1967-97 and is author of *The Geology of Southern Vancouver Island*. He has lived in Victoria since 1976.

1. **Sooke Potholes Provincial Park**. In the scenic Sooke River you see exposed volcanic structures — lava tubes and pillow basalts formed some 56 million years ago, as part of an ancient seafloor.

2. **Newcastle Island Marine Provincial Park**. Late Cretaceous sediments of the Nanaimo Group are well exposed in a beautiful setting that has associations with Nanaimo's history of coal-mining.

3. **East Sooke Regional Park**. Near Creyke Point is a beach that is 25 million years old where the upper part of the Sooke Formation is exposed, with large angular boulders of sedimentary origin forming part of the conglomerate.

4. **The Gulf Islands**. A number of different processes serendipitously came together, such as folding and faulting, glaciation, and northwesterly-directed currents and waves, to produce the northwesterly-aligned physiography of the Gulf Islands.

5. **Botanical Beach Provincial Park**. A wave-cut terrace of Sooke Formation sandstones. The potholes, or tidepools, are carved by sea urchins.

VANCOUVER ISLAND'S
LARGEST LAKES

1. **Kennedy**	69 km^2
2. **Cowichan**	62 km^2
3. **Great Central**	54 km^2
4. **Sproat**	38 km^2
5. **Nimpkish**	36 km^2

Source: Encyclopedia of British Columbia.

BIOGEOCLIMATIC ZONES

The BC Ministry of Forests adapted V.J. Krajina's system of Biogeoclimatic Ecosystem Classification (BEC) to help workers identify site ecology for tree-planting. Vancouver Island is highly varied in altitude, aspect, proximity to the ocean, presence of leeward rainshadow, latitude and other ecological influences. A valuable tool for describing natural resources, BEC was used in the Vancouver Island Land-Use Plan.

Vancouver Island has four of the 14 Biogeoclimatic Zones in BC.

Coastal Western Hemlock (CWH): at lower elevations on either side of the mountains, including the entire northeast coast of the island. The very wet, exposed outer coast is the zone of the temperate rainforest, a mixed species, multi-age ecosystem that often includes old growth and even ancient forest, where individual trees may be more than 1,000 years old. Logging is concentrated in the most productive sites of the CWH Zone.

Mountain Hemlock (MH): subalpine elevations (900 to 1,600 m above sea level) above the CWH. Much of Strathcona Park is in the MH Zone. The MH Zone has short, cool summers and long, cool, wet winters. It's one of Canada's wettest ecological zones — up to 5,000 mm annual precipitation, with as much as 70 percent falling as snow.

Coastal Douglas Fir (CDF): along the southeastern coast and the Gulf Islands, notably drier than more exposed coastline, thanks to the rainshadow of the Vancouver Island and Olympic mountains, with a Mediterranean climate of warm, dry summers. This ecosystem has suffered the most modification. Fire is a factor in its ecology. It's the axis of urbanization and agriculture. The forests handy to tidewater were logged beginning in colonial times. Among its endangered ecosystems is the saanich, where Garry oak and arbutus predominate.

Coastal Mountain-heather Alpine (CMA): the harsh climate of the alpine (beginning at 1,600 m above sea level in the south, lower to the north) is moderated by maritime influences. Above the tree line are a few remnant glaciers and the exposed rock of the extremely rugged central island.

Sources: Ministry of Forests; Biogeoclimatic Zones of British Columbia.

Take 5 FIVE ISLAND TRAILS

1. **Galloping Goose/Lochside Trails:** Victoria to Leechtown and Swartz Bay (90 km), much-loved multi-use railway roadbeds.

2. **Trans-Canada Trail:** Victoria to Nanaimo (200 km), this national multi-use trail is still being assembled through challenging and historic terrain.

3. **West Coast Trail:** Bamfield to Port Renfrew (75 km), a challenging one-week backpacking route along temperate rainforest, sandstone cliffs, waterfalls, caves, sea arches, sea stacks and beaches.

4. **Strathcona Park Ridge Trails:** Many little-marked alpine trails for seasoned backpackers on the granite domes of Vancouver Island's oldest and largest park.

5. **Cape Scott Trails:** A 24 km hike to the northwestern tip of Vancouver Island; many side trips can further extend your hike.

VANCOUVER ISLAND'S PERCENTAGE OF TOTAL AREA IN EACH BIOGEOCLIMATIC ZONE

- Coastal Western Hemlock (CWH): 82.1 percent
- Mountain Hemlock (MH): 10.6 percent
- Coastal Douglas Fir (CDF): 5.2 percent
- Coastal Mountain-heather Alpine (CMA): 2.0 percent

Source: Government of BC.

Douglas fir

The timber industry thrived on logging Douglas fir during the high-lead and railway logging era that started in the early 1900s on Vancouver Island. After World War II, steam-driven donkey engines and carts gave way to diesel power, and chainsaws replaced double-bitted axes and misery whips.

In 1920, almost 2/3 of the wood cut on Vancouver Island was Douglas fir. In 1940 it was still more than 1/2, but by 1960, less than 1/3. The proportion has since risen again as loggers started working in second-growth stands.

The Douglas fir's distinctive orangey wood has long been favored by carpenters for its strength by weight and its dimensional stability; it can be used while still "green."

The tree grows extremely well on the east side of Vancouver Island, where fire is part of the ecosystem. On the coast, the Douglas fir is a pioneer species — after a fire, it tends to form pure, even-aged forests. The tree's thick, corky bark makes it resistant to fire. In a particularly fertile site, the tallest trees can grow to immense sizes — there are records of Douglas firs growing to 125 m in height in BC. The tallest remaining on Vancouver Island stands an estimated 74 m.

A lordly, iconic Douglas fir appears on the crest of the BC Forest Service and on the flag of the fictive nation-state of Cascadia.

DWINDLING OLD-GROWTH

Proportion of original forest cover remaining:

- Of forests 120+ years old, all sites: 45.5 percent
- Of productive old-growth: 25 percent
- Of valley bottom old-growth (where the largest trees grow): 10 percent
- Of old-growth forests on the east side: 1 to 4 percent

Sources: Government of BC and Western Canada Wilderness Committee.

THE RED LIST

- Number of species on BC's "red list" of extirpated, endangered or threatened animals in one or more of the CDF, CMA, CWH and MH zones: 79
- Number of extirpated, endangered or threatened plants: 132
- Number of extirpated, endangered or threatened ecological communities in one or more of the CDF, CWH, MH and CMA zones on Vancouver Island: 51 of 112 communities

Source: BC Conservation Data Centre.

Take 5 FIVE OUTSTANDING
AND ACCESSIBLE NATURAL ATTRACTIONS

1. **Goldstream Provincial Park, near Victoria**. Chum salmon run every November-December.
2. **MacMillan Provincial Park, near Port Alberni**. A large forest of old-growth Douglas fir where you can look to the sky.
3. **Horne Lake Caves Provincial Park**. There are limestone caves — lots of them.
4. **Long Beach section of the Pacific Rim National Park Reserve**. You can't beat the wide open spaces.
5. **Killer whales in Broughton Archipelago**. Charter boats leave from Telegraph Cove.

NATIONAL PARKS

Pacific Rim National Park Reserve comprises three sections with very different features along the 125 km of the west coast between Tofino and Port Renfrew. Long Beach draws thousands to its vast stretches; the Broken Islands are scattered across Barkley Sound; the West Coast Trail winds along a spectacular rocky coast. In all, the reserve protects 290 km^2 of land and 220 km^2 of water.

Endangered Wild Salmon

There are seven species of Pacific salmon in the waters around Vancouver Island. Big **chinooks** (or springs or kings or tyees) are the saltwater sport fisher's favorite. Bright red **sockeye** is historically the most caught and canned; fresh sockeye is favoured by restaurants. **Coho** is fished for both sport and commerce. Feisty **steelhead** are the fly fisher's favorite. (Steelhead and **cutthroat trout** can be both ocean-going and land-locked.) Less glamorous are **chum** (or dog) and **hump-backed pink**, the most plentiful.

Each species has a distinct life cycle within a span of 2 to 8 years. All go to sea and return — mythically, to the same river and even the same patch of gravel — thrashing their way up waterfalls in the relent-less drive to reproduce.

Vancouver Island rivers once teemed with salmon. Some rivers, like the Cowichan, have half a dozen runs. The fish are a vital part of the island's biodiversity. Ecologists refer to salmon as keystone species. Spawning fish lift nutrient-rich biomass into the middle of forested ecosystems. The spawned-out fish die and are eaten by eagles, bears, wolves and countless smaller critters.

Abundant runs were the basis for sizeable commercial fishing indus-tries. Thousands worked and fortunes were made catching, canning and

The Gulf Islands National Park Reserve, one of Canada's newest, protects 15 small islands and many more islets and reefs in the famous archipelago. The land area under protection totals 28 km^2, intertidal areas 8 km2, and marine areas 26 km^2.

Parks Canada also takes care of three National Historic Sites near Victoria: Fisgard Lighthouse (built 1860) Fort Rodd Hill (garrisoned 1878-1956) and Hatley Park (built 1908).

exporting Pacific salmon. Indeed it put British Columbia on the map. The traditional English high tea often included a can of BC salmon. For decades, sports fishers have flocked to Campbell River, Cowichan Bay, Bamfield and other marine centres.

The waters eventually became crowded with competitors. Jostling with the commercial and sports fisheries were Aboriginal fisheries and the various fisheries of Alaska and Washington states. Quotas stayed high until the stocks plummeted in the early 1990's. Habitat destruction has contributed to local declines. Decades of habitat loss resulted from careless and unregulated logging — yarding logs through streams; leaving too little cover to maintain stream temperatures; clearcutting on steep slopes where heavy winter rains trigger avalanches. Habitat has also been lost from dyking, damming, dredging and dumping in streams in urban areas. Critical salmon rearing habitat has been lost in estuaries due to log booming, infilling and other industrial impacts.

As if all that wasn't enough to end the abundance of Pacific salmon, global warming is affecting ocean and river temperatures and the availability of food. The combined effect has been to force the curtailment and even closure of many fisheries.

PROVINCIAL PROTECTED AREAS

BC's first provincial park was Strathcona, created in 1912 and still Vancouver Island's biggest park. The provincial park system has grown until it now includes more than 13 percent of the islands' total area in 122 parks, with no industry allowed across 4,418 km^2 of land and 273 km^2 of water. BC Parks provide a multitude of choices for outdoor recreation, while conserving both small and large ecosystems — some because they are representative and help to maintain biological diversity, others because they are unique.

Ecological reserves are areas set aside for science, education and maintenance of biological diversity. They're even better protected than parks, with permits required to visit many. There are 45 ecological reserves on Vancouver Island and associated islands. They are protecting 71 km^2 of land and 381 km^2 of water.

The BC Government has created five Wildlife Management Areas, totaling 33 km^2, on the island. They're places where intrusive activity is restricted.

(Not to be overlooked for superb recreational value are nearly 50 parks created by Vancouver Island's seven regional districts. The Capital Regional District has assembled the biggest system, with 30 parks protecting 115 km^2.)

Did you know...

that less than 100 km west of Vancouver Island, the Juan de Fuca tectonic plate subducts beneath the North American plate? Their locked energy is released in gigantic megathrust earthquakes (Richter scale 8-9) on average every 500 years, with the last one happening in 1700. Staff at the Pacific Geosciences Centre in Sidney monitor the active zone.

They Said It

The death of a salmon is a strange and wonderful thing, a great gesture of abundance. Yet the dying salmon are not wasted. A whole natural economy is built on their bodies. Bald eagles wait in the trees, bears hunt in the shallows and along the banks, mink and marten and coons come nightly to the feast. All through the winter mallards and mergansers feed in the eddies, and in freshet time, the herring gulls come in to plunge down on the swifter water and pick up the rotting drift. Caddis larvae and other carnivorous insects crawl over the carcasses that are caught in the bottoms of the pools or against the rocks in the eddies. The stream builds its fertility on this death and readies itself to support a new generation of salmon.

– Roderick Haig-Brown writing in *A River Never Sleeps.*

ECOSYSTEMS UNDER STRESS

Vancouver Island's southeast quarter and the Gulf Islands have been discovered by the outside world. With some of the highest average daily temperatures in Canada, almost no snow and much less rain than on the rest of the west coast, what's not to like? There's more. Impossibly scenic vistas. Exquisite landscapes. Twisty redbarked arbutus with shiny green leaves leaning over little shell beaches. Stately Garry oaks in meadows of spring wildflowers — camas, chocolate lilies, shooting stars.

A great part of Vancouver Island's Mediterranean charm comes from the environment. That's why the 250 km coastline between

Did you know...

that a Douglas fir tree on Waterloo Mountain, south of Lake Cowichan, blew down in a storm in the winter of 1985-86, and a count of the rings revealed the tree to be 1,350 years old? Another Douglas fir in the same forest was logged, and there were 1,307 rings on the stump. A yellow cedar stump near Campbell River was found to be 1,636 years old.

Sooke and Campbell River is increasingly urbanized. More than 90 percent of the population lives there. Most of the island's arable land is there, too, and its transportation corridors.

The Nanaimo Lowlands and Southern Gulf Islands ecosections contain some of the most stressed environments in BC. Half of the plant communities are on the Conservation Data Centre's red list of rare, threatened and endangered elements, and more than 25 percent are on the blue list (vulnerable to human activities or natural events).

Hence the East Vancouver Island & Gulf Islands Sensitive Ecosystems Inventory project. The inventory provides scientific data on ecosystem distribution, vegetation, quality and condition that is used in land-use planning. It's the first such inventory to study a large area of BC through a broad, ecosystem approach.

Source: Government of BC.

Did you know...

that Vancouver Island is sometimes called the Island of a Thousand Caves? About 1,200 km^2 (4 percent) of Vancouver Island's surface area is karst (limestone formations). More than 1,000 limestone caves have been documented, and hundreds surveyed since systematic exploration began in the 1970s. Some have more than 10 km of mapped passages. Vancouver Island has more explored caves than all Canadian provinces outside BC combined.

Take 5 VANCOUVER ISLAND'S
LARGEST PROTECTED AREAS

1. **Strathcona-Buttle Lake Provincial Park** 2,458 km^2
2. **Brooks Peninsula Provincial Park** 516 km^2
3. **Pacific Rim National Park Reserve** 290 km^2 + 220 km^2 foreshore
4. **Checleset Bay Ecological Reserve** 15 km^2 + 332 km^2 foreshore
5. **Cape Scott Provincial Park** 223 km^2

Source: BC Parks.

Weblinks

BC Geological Survey Branch's
Geology of Strathcona Provincial Park

A lucid exposition of the complex evolution of the central Vancouver Island mountains.

www.em.gov.bc.ca/mining/geolsurv/Publications/InfoCirc/IC1995-07/default.html

B.C. Conservation Data Centre's "BC Species and Ecosystems Explorer"

A huge database of species that generates lists.

www.a100.gov.bc.ca/pub/eswp/

Graveyard of the Pacific: The Shipwrecks of Vancouver Island

Great stories, great diving.

http://www.pacificshipwrecks.ca/english/index.html

Club Tread's Vancouver Island Community Forum

Useful for getting a line on road closures, local hazards, etc.

www.clubtread.com/sforum/forum.asp?FORUM_ID=32

Weather and Climate

Vancouver Island enjoys some of the best weather in Canada, a never-ending source of smugness for those who live here. Summers can be hot, but most often are comfortably warm and often, without the humidity that plagues much of the country. Winters are cool and wet, but rarely does the temperature dip below freezing unless you're up in the mountains. Spring is long and glorious, starting as early as February and lasting until every bloomin' tree and shrub has put on its annual show. Autumn can begin abruptly with rainy days early in September, but more often than not it's October before Islanders bring out their umbrellas and raincoats.

Two of Vancouver Island's cities, Victoria and Nanaimo, tie for first place in having the most comfortable weather in Canada, according to Environment Canada. The Environment Canada assessment is based on 23 weather categories, including mild winter, spring and fall, few very wet days, abundant sunshine, few hours of fog, smoke and haze, light winds, low humidity, etc.

Two geographical features temper the weather on Vancouver Island — the ocean and the mountains. The Pacific Ocean stabilizes the weather, keeping winters mild and summers cool. The ocean is also the source of the rain and snow. The southern part of Vancouver Island, however, is in the 'rainshadow' cast by the Olympic Mountains to the south, the continental mountains to the east and the coast mountains to the north and west. This means the Greater Victoria region, where almost half of Islanders live, is relatively dry.

Take 5 ANNE MCCARTHY'S TOP FIVE
OBSERVATIONS ABOUT VANCOUVER ISLAND WEATHER

Anne McCarthy finds Vancouver Island weather endlessly fascinating in her job with weather services at Environment Canada. With so much to talk about, she knows someone is bound to say, "But what about … ?" Here's her list anyway.

1. **It doesn't rain all the time everywhere.** The west coast is frequently called the 'Wet Coast'. This is true for some parts of Vancouver Island, but not so for downtown Victoria. Victoria's Gonzales Heights has a normal annual precipitation of 608 mm, which is less than Thunder Bay's 712 mm, Toronto's 792 mm, Ottawa's 944 mm, Montreal's 979 mm and Halifax's 1,452 mm. Major prairie cities have less precipitation — Calgary gets 413 mm, Edmonton gets 483 mm and Saskatoon gets 350 mm, but they lack ocean view property.

2. **It can really rain.** Henderson Lake, between Ucluelet and Port Alberni, for instance set a national record in 1997 for annual total precipitation. It received over 9,300 mm, more than 10 times the rain of downtown Victoria. Gortex is good.

3. **It can snow.** I mean really snow. In Victoria, the more than 60 cm of snow during the Blizzard of '96 is still frequently discussed.

DAILY AVERAGE TEMPERATURES (°C)

Victoria International Airport

Jan	Feb	Mar	Apr	May	Jun	Jul	Aug	Sep	Oct	Nov	Dec
3.8	4.9	6.4	8.8	11.8	14.4	16.4	16.4	14	9.8	6.1	4

Campbell River

Jan	Feb	Mar	Apr	May	Jun	Jul	Aug	Sep	Oct	Nov	Dec
1.3	3	4.8	7.7	11.2	14.2	16.9	16.9	13.4	8.3	4.2	1.7

Stories from that storm are extraordinary, as neighbours shovelled and used sleds to help people needing medical attention, and every man with a front-end loader had instant friends. I learned that jumping off a roof into wet, heavy snow piled almost to the eaves — to retrieve my shovel — is like jumping into a deep vat of cold jello. I had no footing, and had to "swim" out.

4. **It can blow**. On December 15, 2006, Race Rocks just off the Victoria Harbour reported winds to 126 km per hour and with gusts to 158 km per hour. These hurricane force winds cut off power and road access to some of the island's western communities for days. Some exposed areas of North Vancouver Island experience hurricane force winds several times each winter.

5. **Most of the time our weather is temperate**. I feel that spring begins when the first snowdrops bloom — which can be as early as New Year's day, depending on where you live, and summer — well, reliable summer weather really begins July 1st — but sometimes is two weeks late. On the other hand, you can have a rose blooming on Christmas day, as I did in 1999. It wasn't perfect, but I took a picture anyway.

They Said It

AND THE WINNER IS . . .

- Record high: 38.4°C at Port Alberni on August 8, 1978
- Record low: -23.9°C at Campbell River on January 30, 1969
- Record rainfall in one day: 174.2 mm at Tofino on January 2, 1962
- Record snowfall in one day: 73.7 cm in Nanaimo on February 12, 1975
- Record wind speed: 126 km per hour at Race Rocks on December 15, 2006.
- Record wind gust: 159 km per hour in Comox on October 2, 1990
- Record wind chill: -29.7°C in Campbell River on January 5, 1982
- Record humidex: 42.9°C in Nanaimo on August 29, 1974

Source: Based on Environment Canada data from 1971 to 2000 for Victoria, Nanaimo, Comox, Campbell River, Port Hardy, Port Alberni and Tofino.

Did you know...

that the temperature can change substantially between the
waterfront and inland portions of Vancouver Island? On August
12, 1998, for instance, a 10°C difference was measured near
midday between the Victoria waterfront and the Royal Oak-
Beaver Lake area, ten kilometres inland. The greatest difference
— six degrees — was within one kilometre of the waterfront.

IF YOU CAN'T TAKE THE HEAT, MOVE TO THE ISLAND

Vancouver Island is known for its mild winters, but summers are equally temperate. Air conditioning is almost unheard of. Who needs it when the biggest natural air conditioner of all — the Pacific Ocean — is practically on everyone's doorstep?

Out of 100 Canadian cities, Victoria has the 12th coolest summers. Its average daily high is about 22°C for both July and August and evenings cool down to about 11°C. Even in Port Alberni — typically the island's hot spot — summertime highs average around 25°C. Other coastal Canadian cities also have cool summers, such as Corner Brook, Newfoundland, which ranks 9th coolest of 100 centres and Vancouver, which is 10th coolest.

Take 5 FIVE VANCOUVER ISLAND
WEATHER EXPRESSIONS

1. **Pineapple Express:** A sub-tropical air mass from Hawaii that brings warm air and an abundance of moisture to the BC coast.

2. **A 'Qualicum':** A southwest wind that cuts across the island. It is propelled by a difference in pressure between the east and west sides. Refers particularly to those south-westerlies beginning in the Port Alberni inlet and ending just offshore at Qualicum Beach.

3. **An Outflow:** A wind pattern where air from the mainland interior is drawn out across Vancouver Island. To Islanders, it means that in the winter the coldest of airs is coming, and in the summer it means to expect the hottest winds.

4. **An Aleutian Low:** The semi-permanent low-pressure area that sits in the Gulf of Alaska during the winter months and directs frontal systems towards Vancouver Island, sometimes bringing heavy rains.

5. **A Hawaiian High:** It's not a special brand of BC bud, but rather a high-pressure area that builds off the west coast in the summer, producing dry, sunny weather.

FIVE WEATHER FIRSTS
FOR VANCOUVER ISLAND

1. **Greatest precipitation in Canada in a 24-hour period:** 489.2 mm at Ucluelet Brynnor Mines, October 6, 1967.
2. **Greatest precipitation in Canada in one year:** 9,307.3 mm at Henderson Lake, near Port Alberni, on March 17, 1997.
3. **Greatest average annual precipitation in Canada:** 6,655 mm at Henderson Lake.
4. **Greatest average annual precipitation in North America:** 6,655 mm at Henderson Lake.
5. **Least average annual snowfall in Canada:** 20.4 cm at Carnation Creek, which drains into Barkley Sound on the island's west coast.

Sources: The Weather Doctor Almanac, Statistics Canada, and NOAA.

HERE COMES THE SUN

Considering that locals jokingly refer to Canada's west coast as the 'wet' coast, parts of Vancouver Island get a lot of sunshine. Victoria ranks 24th out of 100 Canadian centres as sunniest year-round with 2,086 hours of sunshine. That's way more than Corner Brook, Newfoundland, which places 98th and gets only 1,470 hours of sunshine a year. It's also more than Vancouver, with 1,927 hours (rank 67) but not as much as Canada's sunshine capital, Medicine Hat, Alberta, which comes first with 2,512 hours of sunshine a year.

Sunshine varies widely from place to place on Vancouver Island. Courtenay gets 1,932 hours per year (ranks 62 out of 100), while Campbell River gets only 1,465 hours (99). Duncan and Nanaimo each get about 1,903 hours (76 and 75 respectively) and Port Alberni gets 1,602 hours (95).

Source: Environment Canada.

Did you know...

that during the December 2006 wind storms, some of BC Hydro's customer agents worked 12-hour shifts for 13 days in a row?

Take 5 AVERAGE JANUARY HIGHS
IN FIVE CITIES AT 48° LATITUDE

1. **Victoria, BC:** 6.9°C
2. **Paris, France:** 5.5°C
3. **Vienna, Austria:** 1.1°C
4. **Munich, Germany:** 1°C
5. **Volgograd, Russia:** -5°C

Sources: Environment Canada, Info Please, and Weather.com.

GROWING SEASON

Most communities on Vancouver Island enjoy a cool Mediterranean climate, which means a long growing season but without the heat common to the Okanagan, Ontario, or even the prairies. That means that crops that need a lot of heat, including soybeans, grain corn and field tomatoes are not grown on a large commercial basis.

The number of frost-free days varies considerably from one region to another and even within a region, depending on distance from the ocean. Planting dates are specific to crop and soil conditions but most crops are set by mid-May. In some places where double cropping is possible, the first set dates are earlier. Many vegetable crops are transplants and are not seeded directly into fields, but are started in late winter in greenhouses or cold frames.

Source: BC Agriculture.

Did you know...

that a big tidal range and constricted waterways on the shores of Vancouver Island lead to some of the fastest ocean currents in the world? Water will often flow faster than 30 km per hour.

1. **December 6, 1933:** A violent storm blew in from the Pacific, blowing down thousands of trees and knocking out power and phone service to much of Vancouver Island. Forests around Ladysmith were particularly hard hit.

2. **October 12, 1962:** Typhoon Freda climbed up the coast from California, hitting Victoria with sustained winds of 74 km per hour and gusts of 145 km per hour. A 38-tonne water bomber that was anchored at the Pat Bay airport was ripped from its steel moorings and pushed 200 m across the tarmac. At the Eaton's store in downtown Victoria, two windows shattered, sending Christmas toys whirling into the streets.

3. **December 22, 1996 to January 3, 1997:** Considered the storm of the century, this was actually three storms that pummelled the south part of Vancouver Island and the lower mainland in quick succession, stranding motorists and cutting off transportation for days. In one 24-hour period, 64.5 cm of snow fell at the Victoria airport, the third highest snowfall of any major Canadian city in history. Total losses were tallied at over $200 million.

4. **November 1999 to March 2000:** This wasn't one storm in particular, but a four-month stretch where winds of more than 60 km per hour routinely hammered Vancouver Island, resulting in cancelled ferries and power outages. Victoria got drenched. From December to February, the city received 708.5 mm of precipitation — the most on record. Normal precipitation for the same period would be less than 400 mm.

5. **December 11-15, 2006:** Three powerful storms in a row hit the south coast with winds up to 157 km per hour. In Sooke, part of the roof flew off an apartment building; falling trees were common enough to terrorize residents. In Bamfield and Nitinat, people were without power for more than three days. BC Hydro spent $15.4 million restoring power to almost one-quarter of a million people on the island and the lower mainland.

They Said It

> "Snow does fall in Victoria, pretty much every year in fact, but usually you can treat it like a process server or angry spouse: Lock the doors and ignore it for a few hours and it will go away on its own."
> **– Jack Knox, columnist with the Victoria Times Colonist, March 2, 2008.**

STORMY WEATHER

Vancouver Island can be wet and wild, especially in winter. Storm watching has become a favourite pastime, particularly in Tofino. On the west side of the island, waves bash the shore from December through March, hurling logs and sand high up the beach and keeping all but the best (or the craziest) surfers indoors.

IT'S RAINING, IT'S POURING

Out of 100 centres in Canada, Port Alberni comes second to Prince Rupert as the rainiest city in the country, receiving 1,798 mm of rain per year on average. (Prince Rupert gets 2,469 mm.) If Tofino were included in the 100 centres, it would beat out even Prince Rupert. The town gets 3,257 mm of rain on average each year! What's more, it gets rained or snowed on 206 days of the year.

Port Hardy on the other hand seems almost dry by comparison. It receives only 1,808 mm of rain per year; Campbell River is drier still with 1,344 mm of rain per year. Vancouver Island's 'desert' is Victoria, receiving just 841 mm of rain per year. No wonder native Prickly Pear cacti flourish on nearby Rum Island (officially known as Isle-de-Lis).
Source: Environment Canada.

Did you know...

that a rare but severe electrical storm hit Victoria on August 6, 1997? Lightning struck the Surf Motel on Dallas Road and another bolt hit a car travelling on the Pat Bay highway near Elk Lake.

FOG

With all that rain on some parts of Vancouver Island, and the proximity of the ocean, you might think fog would be common, just as it is on the Atlantic Coast. You'd be wrong. Out of the 100 foggiest cities in Canada, Port Alberni was the foggiest on Vancouver Island, but only placed 43rd, with 30 foggy days per year. Campbell River came in at number 45, Victoria at 66, Duncan at 80, Nanaimo at 81 and Courtenay at 84.

CH-CH-CHILLY

Despite having the mildest of Canadian winters, Islanders still complain about the cold. It may be that we just don't dress for it, but whatever the reason when the thermometer dips below zero, there is a chorus of whining.

The rest of the country understandably has little sympathy for Vancouver Island. Even in winter, temperatures are above zero most of the time. Out of 100 Canadian centres, Victoria has the mildest winter of all. Yellowknife ranks first as the coldest centre in the country, with their average daily January minimum checking in at -31°C. Brr.

- Average daily January minimum in Victoria: 0.7°C
- Average daily January minimum in Comox: 0.4°C
- Average daily January minimum in Port Alberni: -0.5°C
- Average daily January minimum in Campbell River: -2°C

FORGET THE SHOVEL

Victoria gets the least snowfall of 100 centres in Canada — about 44 cm each winter. Duncan comes second at 46 cm. In fact, most urban centres on Vancouver Island are green for much of the winter. Port Alberni is the snowiest spot, receiving about 114 cm per year and Campbell River is not far behind with 109 cm of snow in an average year.

Gander, Newfoundland is Canada's snowiest city out of 100 centres, receiving an average of 443 cm per year of the white stuff.

Source: Environment Canada.

Storm of the Century

When it started snowing in Victoria a few days before Christmas in 1996, everyone looked forward to a Vancouver Island rarity, a white Christmas. Even the weather forecasters could predict at this point that much more was in store for the island.

On Christmas day, arctic air began streaming out of the BC interior and over to the island, lowering temperatures to -8.1°C at the Victoria airport, the lowest ever recorded for that day. It continued to snow for several more days but then the temperature started to rise and the snow became heavier. Over three days, between the 27th and 29th, a total of a 120 cm of snow fell, crippling the Greater Victoria area. BC Transit pulled its buses off the streets, ferry service was cancelled when crews couldn't get to work, and the airport couldn't keep its runways open through all the snow.

With roads impassable and no traffic on the streets, a wonderful peace and quiet descended. Even people living several kilometres from the ocean could hear seals barking. Instead of driving, people took out their cross-country skis. They also helped their neighbours — sharing food and supplies, and shovelling snow for those who couldn't. The snow brought a welcome respite from the real world.

Problem was that then it started to rain. At the airport in Victoria, 50 mm of rain was recorded on the last two days of the year. Roofs that weren't designed for heavy loads started to collapse. Two Viking Air hangers at the airport came down, Vantreight Farms' greenhouses caved in and the roofs on the Thrifty Foods store at Broadmead, the Safeway store in Sidney, the arena at Panorama Leisure Centre and the Royal Bank in Oak Bay were all damaged.

The total cost of the storm was estimated at about $200 million and insurance claims were $120 million — the highest ever for a single weather event in BC. One person died of carbon-monoxide poisoning sitting in his idling car while snow clogged the exhaust pipe. When it was over, it was the worst snowstorm since 1916, but for most of us, it was the best week of winter ever.

PAYING FOR WINTER

In other parts of Canada, the cost of snow removal is a huge expense. Islanders take great pleasure in pointing out that the cost here is minimal. Matter of fact, the city of Victoria has spent only about $150,000 on snow and ice control each year since 2004. The city doesn't even budget for it specifically.

The real cost of winter on Vancouver Island is a result of power outages, usually caused by wind and heavy snow which in turn play havoc with trees and power lines. BC Hydro has budgeted approximately $4.3 million per year since 2001 to restore power after storms. Most years that is still not enough. The winter of 2006-2007 was more expensive by far. BC Hydro spent an unprecedented $36.7 million restoring power after five major storms ravaged coastal communities from October to January.

Source: BC Hydro.

WHITE CHRISTMAS

Don't count on snow for Christmas on Vancouver Island — not unless you're heading up into the mountains. In Victoria, there's only an 11 percent chance of having snow on the ground Christmas Day, and a 'perfect' Christmas — with snow falling and at least two centimetres on the ground — is even less likely, about a seven percent possibility.

Did you know...

that the name 'Cowichan' means 'land warmed by the sun' in the Coast Salish dialect? It's a fitting moniker since the Cowichan Valley receives more than 1,800 hours of sunshine per year on average.

IAN VANTREIGHT'S TOP FIVE
COMPLAINTS ABOUT MOTHER NATURE AND THE WEATHER

Ian Vantreight farms more than 750 acres on the Saanich Peninsula. It is here where his great-grandfather started farming in 1884 after moving to Vancouver Island from Dublin. In 1957, Ian's father started promoting daffodils to raise funds for the Canadian Cancer Society. Today, the Vantreights are the largest grower of daffodils in the country and the second largest in North America. They produce 21 million stems annually. Ian says his father taught him to deal with the weather 'too's'.

1. **It's too hot.** For daffodils, temperature is a big thing. If the temperature in winter is even two or three degrees above normal, we could have daffodils ready for picking in mid-February, when we really want them around Easter. Any earlier than mid-March and it's like buying your Christmas tree in October. There's too much supply and too little demand.

2. **It's too cold.** We had a winter freeze one year that froze the soil deep down and damaged a lot of our bulbs. It was late in the winter, and the bulbs had started to grow, so it was worse than if they had been dormant. We lost 20 percent of our bulbs that year.

3. **It's too wet.** We've put drainage tiles in 300 acres of land, which allows us to get on the land earlier in the spring and stay on later in the fall, but the rest of the land we farm isn't drained. Sometimes the fields get saturated and you can't do anything but wait.

4. **It's too dry.** Fortunately, we've got three large irrigation ponds, so we've never run out of water, but once they're empty of naturally accumulated run-off water then we have to either pump groundwater that is depleting or buy expensive municipal water.

5. **It's too changeable.** We may be having a cold spring, then suddenly it warms up and the crop is ready to pick but we don't have enough workers. You can't find pickers at the drop of a nickel. Or sometimes it turns cold after we've hired pickers and the flowers slow down and now we have too many pickers. There will always be 'too' of something to challenge you if you're farming. You just have to learn how to play the hand as best you can with the cards Mother Nature deals you.

THUNDERSTORMS

If you love watching the sky light up in a thunderstorm, then Vancouver Island is not for you. Nanaimo, Duncan and Victoria rated first, second and third respectively out of 100 centres in Canada as having the fewest days with thunder storms per year, just two or three days each. Campbell River, Port Alberni and Courtenay were also in the top 10 centres with the fewest thunderstorms. In Victoria, that means just three lightning flashes per year on average (per 100 square km). In Windsor, they get 251 flashes per year, the most of any Canadian centre.

SEISMIC CENTRE

Because of its location in the "Pacific Ring of Fire" — an area of active seismic and volcanic activity — Vancouver Island is prone to earthquakes. Lots of them. Quakes that are too small to be felt are an everyday occurrence. Bigger ones — such as the magnitude 7 near Gold River in 1918, and the magnitude 7.3 at Forbidden Plateau, west of Courtenay in 1946 — occur decades apart.

The really big ones, of magnitude 9, happen on average about every 500 years. The last really big one near Vancouver Island — and one of the world's largest earthquakes — was in 1700. The next big one could come any time. Emergency preparedness has greatly increased in the last decade. Many homeowners stash extra food, water and other supplies. Some schools are 'earthquake-proofed' and students practice earthquake drills. New buildings must meet new, higher safety codes.

Sources: Government of BC and Provincial Emergency Program.

Did you know...

that the winter of 1861/62 was one of the coldest and snowiest ever on the south part of Vancouver Island? As many as 900 sheep died in Colwood, livestock were lost in North Saanich, and Victoria's entire inner harbour was covered in a layer of ice thick enough for people to skate on.

Weblinks

Top Ten Weather Story Archives

http://www.msc-smc.ec.gc.ca/media/top10/archive_e.html
With so much weather on Vancouver Island, it's hard to remember which year had all those big storms or when there was no snow for skiing. If it was a memorable event, you'll likely find it in the Top Ten Weather Stories compiled each year by Environment Canada's Senior Climatologist and Canada's foremost weather guru, David Phillips.

The Weather Doctor

http://www.islandnet.com/~see/weather/almanac/arc2004/alm04nov.htm
Keith C. Heidorn, PhD, is 'the weather doctor' and he lives on Vancouver Island, so he can make personal observations about the weather here in addition to providing interesting statistics and stories.

Earthquake Preparedness

http://www.pep.bc.ca/hazard_preparedness/earthquake_preparedness.html
If you live on Vancouver Island you need to be ready for 'the big one'. This provincial government website is loaded with everything you need to know to survive an earthquake.

Did you know...

that Victoria is the only city in Canada west of southern Ontario to receive 50 cm or more of snow in one day? This happened in 1916, 1923 and 1996.

Did you know...

that from February 3, 1988 until November 21, 1993 inclusive, the temperature recorded at Gonzales Heights in Victoria did not fall below zero?

Culture

On Vancouver Island, artistic traditions stretch back thousands of years. The islands possess a cultural vitality that has woven itself into the life of their communities. It's more apparent in a stroll down the street than by scanning listings of concerts and clubs. The islands have the aura of a world apart, close to nature, and on the grid of metropolitan culture more by choice than geography.

Vancouver Island artists and performers generate more than their share of buzz. One local citizen is a genuine jazz great. There are clubs that are magnets for vinyl DJs from around the world. The Victoria Symphony plays to as many as 40,000 people on a raft in the harbour every August. The Cowichan Valley is a centre of slow food culture where world-class chefs get the makings of dinner from their neighbours. The islands probably have the most artists and poets per hectare in Canada — some undoubtedly with *oeuvres* on the immortality track. First Nations keep up proud traditions of art and performance in breathtaking displays in Cowichan, Cape Mudge and Alert Bay.

Local cultures and the cosmopolitan mingle in delightful ways. For example, every summer for 10 days on bucolic Hornby Island, Olsen's Farm plays host to outstanding classical, jazz, folk and world musicians at the Hornby Festival.

Festivals, fairs, markets — that's where many of the islands' cultural communities put their best feet forward. There's a seasonal rhythm; in spring, the celebrations turn to wildlife and nature; summer is the time of music festivals; and fall for food and drink.

THE ARTS WORKFORCE

- Number of artists in Victoria: 860 (2.0 percent of the workforce)
- 100 artisans and craft persons
- 240 musicians and singers
- 160 painters, sculptors and other visual artists
- 40 producers, directors and choreographers
- 255 writers
- Number of artists in Canada: 130,700 (0.8 percent of the workforce)
- Victoria artists' average earnings: $17,800
- Gap between artists' earnings and overall workforce average: 35 percent

SAXOPHONIST PHIL DWYER'S FIVE
PLACES TO TAKE OUT OF TOWN GUESTS

Saxophonist Phil Dwyer is an internationally celebrated jazz musician who has invited some pretty famous friends to visit him at his island home in Qualicum.

1.**French Creek Seafood.** Tammy Moilliet and the rest of the gang at French Creek have everything you need for a seafood feast. I pick and choose from the sea's bounty to make a fisherman's stew with different shellfish, succulent local prawns, ling, halibut, and chunks of spring salmon. Most of the catch at FCS comes into the back of the store from a belt that starts down at the dock. You aren't going to find fresher than that.

2.**Coombs Country Market.** Aside from the kitsch value of the famous "goats on the roof" emporium, the owners and staff at Coombs Country Market are enthusiastic supporters of local BC produce. I buy cases of peaches, cherries, and other delights to can and put away for the winter.

3.**The Old School House Art Gallery.** It really was the old school house when I was a kid here! Now it is an art center that hosts jazz concerts.

4.**Qualicum Heritage Forest.** This 50 acre parcel of old growth forest stands close to the middle of town, and is a testament to the foresight and cooperation of the town's residents. When this parcel was slated to be sold and developed there was a surge of public support to preserve this beautiful forest. Through vigorous fundraising and public awareness campaigns and concerts (I was proud to do one), this spectacular piece of land was saved, untouched, and stands preserved for future generations.

5.**Qualicum Farmer's Market.** From May to October, Saturday mornings are always spent at the downtown Farmer's Market. Produce from Rainbarrel and Blue Heron farms, plump fresh shrimp and prawns from Claire, jams and other delights from Terry's Kitchen and, my favourite, the unbelievable bacon (and other meats) from Sloping Hills Farms. All the farmers, bakers, and artisans at the market put a lot of hard work but also a lot of love and care into what they do and that makes market day a special day for me. Plus it is a great small town way to see friends and introduce out of town guests to everyone.

Take 5 FIVE ISLAND WRITERS
OF NOTE

1. **Essayist: Robert Bringhurst, Quadra Island:** This "Renaissance man" has written 18 books of poetry, three volumes of Haida myths (translated by him), *The Black Canoe* (a study of Bill Reid's famous sculpture), *The Elements of Typographic Style* (a standard text for typographers) and, most recently, two collections of essays, *The Tree of Meaning* (2006) and *Everywhere Being is Dancing* (published in 2007 and winner of a BC Book Prize).

2. **Poet: Carla Funk, Victoria:** From a Mennonite farming background in central BC, she obtained an M.A. in English literature and now teaches at the University of Victoria. Funk was appointed (2006) Victoria's first poet laureate and is a local cultural ambassador. Her latest book of poems is *The Sewing Room* (2006).

3. **Children's writer: Iain Lawrence, Gabriola Island:** A newspaper journalist for 10 years, he quit as editor of the *Prince Rupert Daily News* to work with his sweetheart on a fish farm, turning to writing when that went broke. He has written/edited several books about sailing and 12 fantasy-adventure novels for juvenile readers; *Gemini Summer* (2006) won a Governor General's Award.

4. **Dramatist: Joan MacLeod, Victoria:** MacLeod's plays explore social issues. She wrote *The Shape of a Girl* after the murder of 14-year-old Reena Virk in Victoria to address the issue of girls' cliques. It has now been translated into six languages. Her latest play, *Homechild*, follows the fortunes of two of the 100,000 British children whose caregivers sent then to Canadian farms prior to 1930. She teaches at the University of Victoria.

5. **Fiction writer: Carol Windley, Nanaimo:** A native of Tofino, she has published a novel and two collections of stories (many of them set on Vancouver Island) that explore the dark side of relationships and community. The most recent, *Home Schooling* (2006), won a BC Book Prize and was short-listed for the Giller Prize.

ARTS FUNDING

- The BC Arts Council's 2006 budget: $14 million
- Percentage of BC's arts funding that goes to Vancouver Island: 22
- Number of Vancouver Island communities that received funding: 38

Our Chekhov

Author Alice Munro is one of Canada's most important and respected writers, with 14 books of arresting fiction and memoir. Her disturbing stories, often set on Vancouver Island, have won two Giller prizes and three Governor General's awards. The award winning film *Away From Her* is based on Munro's story, *The Bear Came Over the Mountain*.

Alice Munro and her husband Jim moved to Victoria in 1963. They opened a bookstore where Alice worked part-time while raising her children and trying to find time to write.

When Munro published her first book, *Dance of the Happy Shades*, in 1968, she told the press she had been writing it for 20 years. The book won her a first Governor's General award. Munro has published 14 books and has become one of the most important and respected writers Canada has ever produced.

Munro's success as an author, however, did not translate into domestic bliss. In 1972, Alice and Jim divorced and Alice returned to Ontario to become writer-in-residence at the University of Western Ontario. Alice married Gerald Fremlin in 1976 and the couple moved to a farm outside Clinton, Ontario.

In the early 1990s, Alice and her husband began dividing their time between homes in Clinton and one in Comox. In 2004 Munro explained why she made the move back to the island. "I like the West Coast attitudes," she said. "Winters to me are sort of like a holiday."

Alice Munro has said she never planned to write short stories. She had hoped to create expansive, detailed novels but when she tried to write them she found they just started to sag. Her short stories, which often depict the dilemma of women coming to terms with small town life, are autobiographical in form but not in fact.

The island has more than 20 arts councils. (In comparison, Nova Scotia, with almost 200,000 more people, has 17 communities with arts councils.) The Comox Valley Community Arts Council is one of the oldest, formed in the mid-1960s to increase the emphasis on the

Take 5 MARTIN SEGGER'S FIVE MOST INFLUENTIAL VANCOUVER ISLAND ARTISTS

Martin Segger is the Director of the Maltwood Art Museum and Gallery at the University of Victoria. The Gallery has over 15,000 works of art representing the work of contemporary Western Canadian Artists. Here is his list of Vancouver Island's most influential artists, not including the most obvious and influential of them all, Emily Carr.

1. **Patricia Martin Bates** pioneered the whole idea of the monoprint, the craft of single-edition prints and small runs of individually crafted pierced prints with back lighting. Her art is found in the world's finest art museums including the National Gallery of Canada and the Museum of Modern Art in New York. She was a professor in the Visual Arts department of the University of Victoria for over three decades and was awarded and Honorary Doctor of Fine Arts degree.

2. **Richard Hunt** was born in a First Nations community in Alert Bay. His father, the late Henry Hunt, taught him to carve when he was thirteen. In 1973, he began working at the Royal British Columbia Museum's carving shed with Mungo Martin and quickly became the chief carver. He and his sons created the magnificent Mungo Martin memorial pole at Alert Bay (1971.) In 1991, Richard Hunt received the Order of British Columbia making him the first native artist to be so recognized. In 1994, he received The Order of Canada.

3. **Charles Elliot** is a First Nations carver born on the Tsartlip reserve located in Brentwood Bay. Charles believes you must know about

arts in public schools and develop interest in local art. The council nurtured the Vancouver Island Summer School of the Arts (1966, now known as the Comox Valley Youth Music Centre), the Comox Valley Art Gallery (1973) and the Comox Valley Centre for the Arts (2005).

Sources: Canada Council and CVCAV.

your culture and where it came from before you try to express it in art. He's had an active role in the revival of Coast Salish art by recreating ancient utilitarian art objects and crafting contemporary work within the Coast Salish tradition. His work is found in collections around the world and a Talking Stick he carved was presented to Nelson Mandela.

4. **Michael Morris** is an artist living in Victoria. He was born in 1942 in Saltdean, England. He studied at the Vancouver School of Art in 1962 followed by a year at the Slade School at London University, England. Morris's earliest works were abstracts based upon landscapes and his later work focused on pop culture. His art is housed in major museum collections including the National Gallery of Canada, The Museum of Modern Art, New York and the Ludwig Museum, Cologne. Morris spent the 1980's in Berlin, but returned to Canada in the 1990's.

5. **Myfanwy Pavelic** is a Vancouver Island portait artist. When she was fifteen, Emily Carr arranged for an exhibition of her work. During her adulthood, Pavelic spent part of each year in New York — keeping up with the international art scene. Local and international personalities have been painted by Pavelic, from Prime Minister Pierre Trudeau to Katharine Hepburn. Pavelic's portrait of Yehudi Menuhin was commissioned for Britain's National Portrait Gallery in 1984. She's been awarded the Order of Canada and holds an Honorary Doctorate of Fine Arts from the University of Victoria.

PLACES OF HONOUR

The Order of Canada "honours those who enhanced our country's history and culture" and includes politicians, business and community leaders as well as artists and other cultural workers. It is our nation's highest civilian honour. One hundred seven residents of Victoria have received the honour, as well as nine from Nanaimo, seven from Sidney, five from Comox, and four from Salt Spring Islands. The Order of Canada has been given to 25 other individuals on the island.

CULTURAL SPENDING

Canadians spent $25.1 billion on cultural goods and services in 2005. Victorians spent $310 million, or $1,007 per person — a rate that was second highest of the 15 largest Canadian cities.

LITERATURE

Emily Carr is one of very few artistic geniuses to be favoured in two fields — she won a Governor General's Award with her first published book. Not bad for a self-taught writer, and thankfully more. Late in

Did you know...

that iconic poet Robert Service (author of, among other poems, "The Cremation of Sam McGee") got his start writing poetry for Victoria's *Daily Colonist*?

life, Carr wrote memoirs of a childhood and youth spent close to nature in Victoria. And there's the dyspeptic *The House of All Sorts* (1953). The house in question was a small apartment block Carr built on a corner of her family property. In the depression before World War I it became a rooming house.

"I was not nailed, I was screwed into the House of All Sorts, twist by twist," she wrote. "Every circumstance, financial, public, personal, artistic, had taken a hand in that cruel twirling of the driver. My screws were down to their heads. Each twist had demanded— 'Forget you ever wanted to be an artist. Nobody wanted your art. Buckle down to being a landlady.'"

One of the island's literary lights today is Wendy Morton, a poet and sometime private investigator in Sooke. The *doyenne* of long-running open-mike poetry evenings (Fridays at the Black Stilt Café in Victoria), Wendy is chief instigator of the annual Random Acts of Poetry day, where you're likely to be approached on the street or on a bus to be read a poem. Wendy was appointed the WestJet "poet of the sky." She would make up occasional poems for passengers bound for births, weddings, funerals, reunions, what-have-you.

LITERARY EXCELLENCE

These Islanders (some adoptive; some part-time; some who have moved on) won the Governor General's Literary Award:

Emily Carr, *Klee Wyck* (non-fiction, 1941)

Lorna Crozier, *Inventing the Hawk* (poetry, 1992)

Dave Godfrey, *The New Ancestors* (fiction, 1970)

Jack Hodgins, *The Resurrection of Joseph Bourne* (fiction, 1979)

Bruce Hutchison, *The Unknown Country* (non-fiction, 1942); *The Incredible Canadian* (non-fiction, 1952); *Canada: Tomorrow's Giant* (non-fiction, 1957)

Robert Kroetsch, *The Studhorse Man* (fiction, 1969)

Patrick Lane, *Poems New and Selected* (poetry, 1978)

Iain Lawrence, *Gemini Summer* (children/youth fiction, 2007)

Joan MacLeod, *Amigo's Blue Guitar* (drama, 1991)

Don McKay, *Night Field* (poetry, 1991); *Another Gravity* (poetry, 2000)

Alice Munro, *Dance of the Happy Shades* (fiction, 1968); *Who Do You Think You Are?* (fiction, 1978); *The Progress of Love* (fiction, 1986)

P.K. Page, *The Metal and The Flower* (poetry, 1954)

Kit Pearson, *Awake and Dreaming* (children/youth fiction, 1997)

Pamela Porter, *The Crazy Man* (children/youth fiction, 2005)

Al Purdy, *The Cariboo Horses* (poetry, 1965); *The Collected Poems* (poetry, 1986)

Leon Rooke, *Shakespeare's Dog* (fiction, 1983)

Take 5 — FIVE ISLAND
ARTISTS/CRAFTERS

1. **Ted Harrison** is a Victoria painter and maker of popular prints and posters. His subjects include Canada's north, where he lived for many years.

2. **Robin Hopper** is a potter in Metchosin who, with his partner Judi Dyelle, displays both artistic work and utility wares in a stunning garden setting, amid old-growth Douglas fir trees.

3. **Tony Hunt, Jr.** is a carver and a dancer in the Kwakwaka'wakw tradition. His father is hereditary chief of the KwaGulth First Nation; his great grandfather was Mungo Martin. His carved and painted masks are prized by collectors the world over. Works are on display at Alcheringa Gallery, 665 Fort St, Victoria.

4. **Carole Sabiston** is a fibre artist in Victoria whose large hangings and theatre sets are admired world-wide. A good place to see her work is on the walls of Munro's Books, 1108 Government St, Victoria.

5. **Godfrey Stephens** is a legendary Victoria painter, sculptor and boatbuilder whose monumental abstract columns, carved of red and yellow cedar, can be seen at the entrance to the Victoria Press Building, 2621 Douglas Street. His carving Kluk Chitl is in Swan's Hotel pub, 506 Pandora Ave.

Carol Shields, *The Stone Diaries* (fiction, 1993)
Stephen Scobie, *McAlmon's Chinese Opera* (poetry, 1980)
Phyllis Webb, *The Vision Tree: Selected Poems* (poetry, 1982)
Jan Zwicky, *Songs for Relinquishing the Earth* (poetry, 1999)
Source: Canada Council.

CITY OF VICTORIA BUTLER BOOK PRIZE
- 2004: Kevin Patterson for *Country of Cold.*
- 2005: Terrence Young for *After Goodlake's.*
- 2006: Mark Zuehlke for *Holding Juno.*
- 2007: Bill Gaston for *Gargoyles.*

ARTS & CRAFTS
In the 1890s serious would-be artists like Emily Carr and Sophie Pemberton went elsewhere to train — San Francisco, London and Paris. Carr moved to Vancouver and exhibited her work there without success. By 1910 Victoria established its first modest outlet for local artists to show their work, the Island Arts and Crafts Society.

By the 1920s, Group of Seven painter Fredrick Varley was teaching in Vancouver and began taking his classes out to the island's west coast. The beginnings of a modernism of the island can be traced to Emily Carr's friendship with Seattle artist Mark Tobey in the same period.

Today the islands' art scene is flourishing. Many First Nations artists enjoy international fame. They balance the creative with respect for tradition in carved and painted work that is accessible and endlessly fascinating. For exposure to the art of the Metropolis, look no further than the Art Gallery of Greater Victoria. In 2008 it mounted a major exhibit of Andy Warhol's work.

On the craft side, many talented potters and weavers take traditional techniques into new forms in one-of-a-kind productions.

CLASSICAL MUSIC

Where else can you hear an orchestra play variations on a Triathlon? "Mind over Mountain," by sensational Victoria-based composer Tobin Stokes, had its premiere performance by the Victoria Symphony in 2006, while he was composer-in-residence. Tania Miller, the symphony's conductor and music director, has found new ways to mix fun and serious music. Established in 1941, the symphony performs 100 concerts a year, most notably at the Symphony Splash, an annual event on the Inner Harbour where the orchestra plays on a barge to hundreds of kayakers and small boaters and the thousands who sit on the lawns of the Parliament Buildings and Empress Hotel.

Nanaimo's Vancouver Island Symphony, under artistic director Pierre Simard is in its 14th season playing at the Port Theatre and other venues up-island.

The Sooke Philharmonic is a full-size semi-professional orchestra conducted by its founder, Norman Nelson, with 6 programs a season, plus a mid-summer Fling, an open-air pop concert.

Victoria Conservatory of Music, established in 1964, instructs 2,000 students (full-time and casual) and is renowned for its exacting standards, with alumni of the calibre of Richard Margison. The conservatory is housed in a heritage church whose sanctuary became the 800-seat Alix Goolden Performance Hall, with the best acoustics in town.

The School of Music at the University of Victoria produces musicians of international stature. The faculty includes the members of the Lafayette String Quartet, established by four women in 1986 and still performing as artists-in-residence.

They Said It

"Be careful that you do not write or paint anything that is not your own, that you don't know in your own soul."

– Emily Carr

MUSICAL HOMES

Vancouver Island is the birthplace to a number well-known musicians — music producer David Foster, pop singer Nelly Furtado, rock bassist Bryce Soderberg — all from Victoria — and jazz artist Diana Krall from Nanaimo. Diana Krall married singer/songwriter Elvis Costello in 2003, and they divide their time between New York City and a home in Nanoose Bay.

Singer/songwriter Sarah McLaughlin has a beach house in Tofino. Raffi Cavoukian, children's entertainer, has a home on Mayne Island. Randy Bachman and Valdy both call Salt Spring Island home.

Go Nelly!

Nelly Kim Furtado, named after Soviet gymnast Nellie Kim, was born in Victoria on December 2, 1978, to Portuguese immigrants Maria Manuela and António José Furtado. By the age of four, young Nelly was singing publicly with her mother. Indeed throughout her early years, her attention moved from singing to playing instruments such as the trombone, ukulele, guitar and keyboards. She started writing songs at age 12.

In October 2000, she released her first album, *Whoa, Nelly!* It became an international success, spawning hit singles such as "I'm Like a Bird" and "Turn off the Lights." To date, the album has sold over 5 million copies. She followed up with *Folklore* in 2003. Many critics blame the lack of commercial success of *Folklore* to her noticeably less "poppy" sound.

After taking some time off to have a daughter, Furtado was back. In 2006, she released *Loose*, which again put her on top of the international music scene. She has collaborated with the likes of Timbaland, Justin Timberlake and Keith Urban, garnered seven Grammy Award nominations and won five Junos. She enjoys a worldwide reputation for innovation by continuously experimenting with different instruments, sounds, genres, languages, and style.

SOME OF THAT JAZZ

Fraser MacPherson (1928-1993) was a Victoria jazz musician who played the saxophone, clarinet and flute. For years, he was a favourite on CBC radio's Jazz Radio-Canada and Jazz Beat. In 1978, he made the first of four tours through the USSR. He was awarded the Order of Canada in 1987 for bringing an awareness of Canadian jazz musicians outside Canada's borders.

Diana Krall has put Vancouver Island jazz on the map. The virtuoso pianist and singer/songwriter, born in Nanaimo in 1964, was discovered as a teenager playing clubs in Nanaimo. In 1983 legendary bass player

Bio KING OF POP

Born to a large family in Victoria in 1949, David Foster's musical talents quickly became apparent. Foster began studying piano at the age of five, and his family nurtured his gifts and ambition. He was enrolled as a student at the University of Washington at the age of 13, and three years later accepted the offer to join the backing band for Chuck Berry. In Canada, he did apprentice keyboard work with Tommy Banks and Ronnie Hawkins. With Victoria singer-songwriter B.J. Cook he formed the band Skylark. Their song Wildflower, written by guitarist Doug Edwards and Dave Richardson, a Saanich police officer, and produced by Capital Records, was a hit in 1972.

Foster established a reputation as a studio session keyboardist in Los Angeles. He won his first of 14 Grammys for co-writing After the Love Has Gone, the 1979 Earth, Wind & Fire hit. He became sought-after as a movie songwriter and soundtrack producer. But it was in producing records that Foster's signature sound emerged — the torchy ballads of Natalie Cole (Unforgettable, 1991) Whitney Houston (I will Always Love You, 1993), Céline Dion (The Power of Love, 1994) and many others.

Foster's success as a producer is without peer, prompting *Time Magazine* to anoint him "the true King of Pop" in 1994. He was appointed a vice-president of Atlantic Records the same year. He has

Ray Brown, who backed Dizzie Gillespie and Oscar Peterson and married Ella Fitzgerald, visited a bar where Krall was playing and convinced Krall's mother that Diana had a future in performance. She moved to Los Angeles and went on to win over light jazz audiences everywhere. A two-time Grammy Award winner, Krall is an Officer of the Order of Canada.

Saxophonist Phil Dwyer, an internationally-celebrated musician who has performed with Red Rodney, Renee Rosnes, Kenny Barron, Tom Harrell, Aretha Franklin and Ian Tyson, teaches at Malaspina College and produces the annual Jazz in the Garden Concert at Milner Gardens in Qualicum Beach. Dwyer believes it is the island's strong tradition of musical instruction that has produced jazz artists like Krall.

nurtured the careers of such up-and-coming singers as Michael Bublé and Josh Groban. Among his many honours are the Order of British Columbia, the Order of Canada and, in 2007, induction into the Canadian Music Industry Hall of Fame.

Foster has burned his share of bridges although he also builds them. He has been a tireless producer and performer at charitable events.

The story is told that one day in 1986, David's mother called from Victoria to ask him to visit a child who was in LA having a liver transplant. The experience was moving for Foster. His response was to start the David Foster Foundation which provides Canadian families with financial assistance to support their children through the rigors and trauma of organ transplant surgery. The Foundation, based in Victoria, has helped nearly 400 families across Canada.

Foster's variety-show fundraisers with his talented friends are an institution in their own right. After drawing on Victorians' generosity for 18 years, they went national in 2007. A fundraiser in Calgary made the Foundation $3 million.

David Foster currently lives in Santa Monica. Does he ever return to his home town? Half a dozen times in a recent three-month period.

FOOD AND DRINK

This is a land of good food and drink. With some 300 dining establishments, Victoria reportedly has the second most restaurants per capita in North America. When in Sooke, one can choose *la haute cuisine* of the island's most renowned dining room, Sooke Harbour House, operated by Sinclair and Fredrica Philip, or the friendly ambience of Mom's

Take 5 FIVE WONDERFUL CUPS OF TEA

Tearooms serve up pots of their own specialty blends accompanied by sandwiches and pastries. Although the tradition arrived on the island with the coming of the Hudson's Bay Company, Islanders and island establishments have given it their own twist.

1. **The Fairmont Empress, Victoria.** You would be forgiven for thinking Afternoon Tea was invented here. The tradition is so firmly ensconced in this grand old hotel that Canadians across the country know the hotel as much for its tea as its old world charm. The Empress turned the century mark in 2008 and the tea and little sandwiches are as delightful as ever.

2. **Milner Gardens & Woodland, Malaspina College.** When the Queen of England raves about the tea you know you are on track. Milner Gardens is also the place that *Canadian Geographic Travel* calls one of the ten best public gardens in Canada.

3. **Calico Cat Tea House, Nanaimo.** This teahouse not only offers fine tea and traditional scones and tea but tea leaf readings by professional readers.

4. **Abkhazi Garden and Tea Room, Oak Bay.** The original owners of the stunning property, the Abkhazis, settled on the island after being told one could as eccentric as one wanted to be. That eccentricity thankfully continues unabated.

5. **White Heather Tea Room, Oak Bay.** A favourite with the locals, and the locals know their tea. The tea itself is innovative while staying true to its traditions. Bring a big appetite for the Big Muckle Tea.

Take 5

ROBERT BATEMAN'S FIVE
MOST INSPIRING ISLAND LOCALES

Robert Bateman moved from southern Ontario to Salt Spring Island after a visit west over 20 years ago. "I asked myself, why am I still living in purgatory when I could be living in paradise," he says. The renowned wildlife artist and environmentalist has had his work exhibited at the Smithsonian Museum of Natural History in Washington, DC, the Canadian Embassy in Tokyo and the Art Gallery of Greater Victoria. Bateman has explored the Island extensively with scientists and environmental activists.

1 **The Bunsby Group of Islands.** With its craggy shoreline of low cliffs, arches and caves, this ecological reserve on a wild section of the west coast of northern Vancouver Island protects a colony of sea otters. This affluent biotic zone with all the abundance of intertidal life is vulnerable to oil spills, industry, and, more recently, the press of tourism.

2. **Helliwell Park on Hornby Island.** Hornby Island is known as a place where artists can find peaceful inspiration, and Helliwell Park is considered by many to be the island's heart. With its variety of meadows, cliffs over the sea and deep forests, it is a magical place where everything comes together.

3. **Salt Spring Island.** Inspiration comes, of course, from travels, but most comes from around home. There is a place in the center of the island with a huge broadleaf maple, deep mossy woods and sword ferns. Nearby there are hilltops covered with Garry Oaks and Arbutus trees.

4. **Tofino.** What is most precious about this region is the connection between the land and the water. If you are lucky enough to be able to go out in a zodiac and explore the coast off Vargas Island, you can't help but be inspired by the smell of the wind and the variety of life, all combining to make this the best part of the earth.

5. **Royal Roads University, Victoria.** Natural heritage and human heritage are getting wiped out faster than ever before, but at Royal Roads, early European history blends with an old growth forest — something that mirrors my own belief in the importance of conserving natural and human history.

Café, with its working jukebox.

Vancouver Island has emerged as a center of Slow Food. Established in Italy to counteract the global Fast Food trend, the Slow Food movement focuses on using sustainable local ingredients with a dual goal of preserving both regional specialties and local biodiversity. Epicures and pilgrims now flock to the island in search of culinary nirvana.

In 2001, Sinclair Philip and Mara Jernigan, chef of Fairburn Farm, near Duncan, established the Vancouver Island and Gulf Islands Slow Food Convivium, a loose association of 100 chefs, restaurateurs, farmers and environmentalists, to celebrate Vancouver Island's regional cuisine.

Eric Pateman, founder of Edible BC, an Internet retailer of local artisan foods, says the new cuisine consists of old world ingredients prepared with new thinking. The result is true island fare that can be found in restaurants throughout the islands.

Salmonberry jam, bull kelp pickles, artisan cheeses aged in local port and locally farmed oysters are just some of the delicacies.

FARM MARKETS
Brentwood Bay: Saturday, June-October
Cedar: Sunday, May-October
Duncan: Saturday, April-October
Errington: Saturday, May-September

Esquimalt: Wednesday, May-September
Ganges, Salt Spring Island: Saturday and Tuesday, April-October
Luxton Station, Langford: Saturday, June-October
Metchosin: Sunday, May-October
Moss Street, Victoria: Saturday, May-October
Nanaimo: Friday, April-October
Qualicum Beach: Saturday, May-October
Sidney: Thursday, June-August
Sooke: Saturday, May-September
Vic West: pocket markets Wednesday, year-round

Take 5   FIVE PUBS
TO KNOCK BACK A COLD ONE

Public houses date back to Fort Victoria and were a place where a weary traveler could get a meal and a pint. The pub culture continues to be alive and well on the island.

1. **Irish Times Pub, Victoria:** With live celtic music and kilt-wearing servers, this pub will make patrons think they've taken a trip back to the old country.
2. **Shady Rest Pub, Qualicum Beach:** This beachfront pub with its stunning views has been a favourite place for sundowners for 75 years.
3. **Crow & Gate Pub, Yellowpoint:** A cozy English pub set in a delightful garden is simply the place you must visit if you have that hankering for roast beef and Yorkshire pudding.
4. **Dinghy Dock Pub, Protection Island/Nanaimo:** A picturesque floating restaurant/bar that you can arrive at on your own boat or by ferry.
5. **Craig Street Brew Pub, Duncan:** This brew pub serves up craft pints, including A Fools Ale, Bee Cool Honey Lager and Chocolate Cherry Porter. The modern day pints contrast well with the old fashioned feel — the bar and paneling that came from a 1906 Montreal hotel.

WINE AND SPIRITS

Vancouver Island and the Gulf Islands have become known as the Wine Islands in recent years. While grapes have been growing in the Okanagan for a few decades, it took longer for islanders to embrace the idea — the belief was the region's mild, rainy climate wouldn't work for grape growing. It turned out that several early ripening grapes thrive on the island and the region's *terroir* has been compared to Alsace and Chablis.

- The first winery on Vancouver Island opened in 1992.
- There are currently 32 wineries, cideries and meaderies, and three distilleries on seven islands.
- In 2006, 357 island acres were planted with grapes accounting for just over 5 percent of BC's total.
- During the last weekend in September, the Cowichan Wine and Culinary festival offers tastings at a number of the wineries.

- Vancouver Island's specialty wine is Wild Blackberry Desert Wine. Cherry Point Vineyards in Cobble Hill makes one popular version.
- Venturi-Schulze Vineyards in Cobble Hill markets a superb balsamic vinegar, not cheap.

Source: Wine Islands.

Cougars Drink from The Cup

Oak Bay was the venue of the first professional hockey game played west of the Great Lakes, on January 3, 1912. Onto Canada's first artificial ice surface skated Lester Patrick. He owned the local team and was its playing coach and captain. A rushing defencemen — one of the first — Patrick naturally scored the first goal of the game.

Patrick's sawmilling family also built arenas on the mainland and established a three-team league. Patrick's team was named the Senators, then the Aristocrats, and (briefly during World War I) played in Spokane, WA as the Canaries. As the Victoria Cougars, they competed in a new Western Canada Hockey League in 1918-19.

The National Hockey League was still a novelty in 1925 when the powerful Montreal Canadiens took the train west for the five-game Stanley Cup series. On their roster were the dazzling young forward Howie Morenz and the legendary goalie Georges Vézina. Three games were to be played by western rules, which allowed forward passing in the centre zone and changes on the fly. The Cougars skated rings around the Canadiens and won the series three games to one. It was the last time a non-NHL team was invited to compete for the Cup.

When the western league folded, Patrick went on to manage the New York Rangers. After retiring in 1947, he started a new Victoria Cougars team, playing in the Western Hockey League.

Known as the Silver Fox, Lester Patrick (1883-1960) is one of hockey's greats.

ISLAND SPORTING EXCELLENCE

Steve Nash is a point guard with the Phoenix Suns of the NBA. Brought up in Victoria, he is a two-time NBA Most Valuable Player and considered one of the best players to ever play the game. Nash was named an Officer of the Order of Canada in December 2007. The Steve Nash Charitable Foundation opened a BC office in 2007. Since that time it has provided grants to youth-focused organizations such as the Power To Be Adventure Therapy in Sidney and the Victoria Youth Clinic. When Nash played for Canada at the last Olypmics, he is rumoured to have given each of his teammates $10,000. His modesty and sincerity have won him fans all over the world.

Port Alberni born Rick Hansen injured his spine in a car crash and

Did you know...

that Ian Tyson, half of the legendary 60s folk duo Ian & Sylvia, was born and raised in Victoria? Tyson has raised cattle on his Alberta ranch since the 1970s and is an active singer/songwriter.

Take 5 — FIVE TERMS YOU'LL HEAR
ON THE BEACH IN TOFINO

Tofino is the surfing capital of Canada. A dozen or so surf shops teach lessons and outfit visitors for the year round sport. Even Pierre Trudeau carved a wave back in the day.

1. **Dropping in:** Catching a wave that is already occupied by another surfer.
2. **Cox Bay:** The beach that usually has the biggest surf, about 10 km out of Tofino.
3. **Grommet:** A young surfer.
4. **Longboard:** A surfboard that is usually over nine feet in length. Because of their size they are easier for beginners to learn on.
5. **Peak:** Part of a wave that rises and breaks first.

Source: Tourism Tofino.

was confined to a wheelchair when he was only 15 years old. He didn't let the injury stop him, however, and became the first student with a physical disability to graduate in Physical Education from the University of British Columbia. He went on to win number of wheelchair marathons, before launching his Man in Motion world tour, a 40,000 km trek through 34 countries. The tour not only galvanized the country but also the world. It raised more than $26 million for spinal cord injury research. The Man in Motion tour was immortalized by the song "St. Elmo's Fire (Man in Motion)" by another Islander, David Foster. In 1987, Hansen was appointed a Companion of the Order of Canada.

Weblinks

Nanaimo Cultural Capital

http://www.nanaimoculturalcapital.ca

This website details the activities and events of the Nanaimo Cultural Capital program.

Wine Islands Vintners Association

http://www.wineislands.ca

Check this site for winery information, touring maps and festival information.

Slow Food Vancouver Island & Gulf Islands

http://www.slowisland.ca

This website introduces the movement and gives information about slow food events.

Economy

Natural resources have always been the foundation of Vancouver Island's economic life. First Nations enjoyed a rich lifestyle based on the bounty of the sea and forest. Early settlers, bent on farming, found land-clearing a gargantuan task. For the average family on the land — which briefly included most Islanders — economic life was a seasonal round of farming, logging, fishing, hunting, trapping, prospecting, weaving . . . whatever would bring sustenance or a little revenue.

The first big resource industry on the island was mining, and indeed coal was king for nearly a century. Nanaimo was literally built on coal — the seams and tunnels ran right under the centre of town. Thousands worked underground there as well as in new deposits found in Wellington, Cumberland and Extension.

Early logging furnished spars for sailing ships and lumber for local construction, but industrial forestry dates from the early 20th century, when the power of steam was harnessed. For about half a century (1940-1990), forestry was king, and it was said that "50 cents of every dollar" came from wood. Today forestry is in a tailspin, with markets drying up and costs skyrocketing. Logging operations and mills are closing. Once-flourishing fisheries are depleted from overfishing, and whole fleets of fishboats sit on blocks.

Outside of the resource industries, Vancouver Island's economy is booming. It continues to diversify, confounding and surprising even those who predicted it would happen. The world finds new reasons to beat a path to Vancouver Island's door. The red-hot housing market and construction boom reflect the region's popularity as a place to live. Skilled young high-technology workers and retired baby-boomers alike are attracted by its beauty and relaxed lifestyle, not to mention the mild winters.

Clusters of industries trade on Vancouver Island's mystique of health, spirituality and art. With new and established markets in every direction, the island is no longer Canada's most westerly terminus, but rather at the center of new and established markets.

GROSS DOMESTIC PRODUCT
- BC GDP at market prices (2006): $158,335 million
- Change from previous year: +3.3 percent
- BC GDP per capita: $36,649
- Change from previous year: +1.9 percent
- Canada GDP per capita: $39,272
- Change from previous year: +1.7 percent

Source: BC Statistics.

TAXES (2008)
- Provincial sales tax: 7 percent
- GST (federal sales tax): 5 percent
- Personal income tax rate: 5.24 percent to 14.7 percent
- Small business tax rate: 4.5 percent
- Corporate tax rate: 12 percent

Sources: Ministry of Small Business and Revenue and Canada Revenue Agency.

Did you know...

that the total annual timber cut on the BC coast peaked at 27.8 million m^3 in 1980? The long-term sustainable yield is projected to be 17 million m^3.

TAX FREEDOM DAY

The date (2007) in which earnings no longer go to taxes:

Alberta	June 1
New Brunswick	June 14
Prince Edward Island	June 14
Manitoba	June 16
British Columbia	**June 16**
Ontario	June 19
Nova Scotia	June 19
Saskatchewan	June 22
Quebec	June 26
Newfoundland and Labrador	July 1

Source: The Fraser Institute.

INFLATION

Average inflation rate 1997-2007:

- In BC: 1.8 percent
- In Canada: 2.1 percent

PERSONAL INCOME

- Provincial per capita income (2006): $32,600
- Change from previous year: +6.0 percent
- National per capita income: $33,530
- Disposable (after taxes) per capita income in BC: $25,364
- Disposable (after taxes) per capita income in Canada: $25,798

Source: BC Statistics.

Did you know...

that Lighthouse Brewing Company, a microbrewery that produces Race Rocks Amber, Beacon IPA, Keepers Stout, and Lighthouse Lager, is found in over 450 retail stores and on taps across British Columbia? The company was started in 1998.

"There's definitely enough cyclists here to support [a new bicycle shop]. Just outside our door here, we counted 35 bikes in under an hour, and that's only going to increase when they connect the E&N rail line trail to the Galloping Goose in 2010."

– Bill Fry, on opening Trek Victoria Pro City Cycle, the 26th bike shop in the city.

HOUSEHOLD INCOME

Median total income from Statistics Canada's latest available data:

Ottawa	$80,300
Calgary	$75,400
Victoria	$66,900
Quebec City	$64,900
Halifax	$64,700
Toronto	$61,800
Winnipeg	$61,600
Vancouver	$58,800
Montreal	$58,600

BY THE HOUR

Average hourly earnings, all industries, BC (2007): $19.11

Change in last 10-year period: +2.9 percent

Proportion of jobs paying:

Less than $10.00	16.3 percent
$10.00-$14.99	21.1 percent
$15.00-$19.99	23.6 percent
$20.00-$24.99	16.6 percent
$25.00 or more	22.4 percent

Source: Statistics Canada.

You Said How Much?

Average hourly wages for Vancouver Island based on the latest available data.

Pharmacists	$45.26
Physicists and Astronomers	$45.19
Civil Engineers	$43.64
Commercial Divers	$35.00
University Professors	$33.81
Registered Nurses	$29.96
Construction Managers	$29.65
Senior Managers (Health, Education, Social Services)	$28.64
Supervisors, Logging and Forestry	$28.47
Secondary School Teachers	$28.42
Longshore Workers	$28.07
Software Engineers	$27.84
Contractors and Supervisors, Carpentry Trades	$27.21
Deck Officers, Water Transport	$25.70
Heavy-Duty Equipment Mechanics	$25.41
Biologists and Related Scientists	$24.54
Social Workers	$24.46
Financial Managers	$24.23
Financial Auditors and Accountants	$23.95
Sawmill Machine Operators	$23.18
Sales, Marketing and Advertising Managers	$22.80
Forestry Technologists and Technicians	$22.20
Bus Drivers and Other Transit Operators	$20.00
Secretaries (Except Legal and Medical)	$19.85
Conservation and Fishery Officers	$19.83
Motor Vehicle Body Repairers	$18.19
Customs, Ship and Other Brokers	$18.00
Land Surveyors	$17.96
General Office Clerks	$16.78
Bookkeepers	$16.59
Receptionists and Switchboard Operators	$15.68
Accommodation Service Managers	$15.39
Retail Trade Managers	$15.00
Visiting Homemakers, Housekeepers, etc.	$14.85
Program Leaders/Instructors in Recreation and Sport	$14.66
Restaurant and Food Service Managers	$14.50
Fish Plant Workers	$14.34
Cooks	$12.82
Security Guards and Related Occupations	$12.28

Source: Service Canada.

WHERE THE MONEY GOES
Monthly cost of living for a family of four in Victoria (2008):

	$	% of total
Shelter	1,299	28.1
(3-bedroom unit, telephone, utilities, contents insurance)		
Child care	947	20.5
Food	619	13.4
Transportation	497	10.8
Clothing	192	4.2
Emergencies	191	4.1
Health expenses (non-MSP)	133	2.9
Medical Services Plan (MSP) health insurance	108	2.3
Parent education	83	1.8
Other	547	11.8
(personal care items, household supplies and furnishings, small appliances, recreation, laundry, banking, computer, internet, children's toys)		
Total	4,616	

Source: Quality of Life Challenge.

BUYING A HOUSE

Average house prices as of February 2008.

Victoria	$588,826
British Columbia	$478,172
Alberta	$359,953
Ontario	$304,322
Quebec	$210,826
Saskatchewan	$209,702
Nova Scotia	$188,110
Manitoba	$173,809
Newfoundland and Labrador	$151,244
New Brunswick	$143,207
Prince Edward Island	$131,594

Source: Canadian Real Estate Association.

Average price of a single-family home in Greater Victoria:

1978	$63,733
1988	$127,888
1998	$246,018
2008 (Feb)	$588,826

Source: Victoria Real Estate Board.

THE HIGH COST OF ISLAND LIVING

Islanders routinely complain about the higher cost of living here compared to the mainland....everything from the price of food to the price

Take 5 ANDREW DUFFY'S FIVE
ISLAND ECONOMIC TRENDS

Andrew Duffy is a business writer for the *Victoria Times Colonist*. He was born in Glasgow, Scotland and has lived on Vancouver Island for 21 years.

1. The massive growth of high-tech industry on southern Vancouver Island, to the point where, with annual revenues of $1.7 billion, it has eclipsed tourism as the largest non-resource-based industry.

2. Tourism remains healthy on the south island. The trade grew by four percent last year and will likely grow by three percent this year, bucking the trend across Canada, where there have been significant declines, particularly in the US market. The number of US travelers to BC dropped 6.5 percent last year.

3. A massive construction boom has created one of the lowest unemployment rates in Canada and is restrained only by the labour shortage (a problem all over BC and Alberta).

4. Culinary tourism is a niche market that has ties with the slow-food movement. There has been a big marketing push highlighting island wineries and restaurants, some of which, like Rosemeade Dining Room, have garnered rave reviews across Canada.

5. Golf tourism is on the upswing with the construction of two Jack Nicklaus-designed courses at Bear Mountain, attracting high-yield visitors who tend to spend a lot of money. The island's golf courses have seen the light and have increased their marketing to attract more visitors.

Take 5 — FIVE MOST EXPENSIVE HOMES
ON THE MARKET ON VANCOUVER ISLAND

1. **$29 million**, Oak Bay, (highest price listed in Canada)
2. **$18.5 million**, Central Saanich (5th highest in Canada)
3. **$15.5 million**, North Saanich, (9th highest in Canada)
4. **$15 million**, Oak Bay
5. **$14.95 million**, Central Saanich

Source: MLS April 2008.

of gas. But the price of housing, especially in Victoria, elicits the biggest groans. In early 2008, the average price of a single-family home in Greater Victoria was $588,826. Only 1 city in Canada, Vancouver, was more expensive.

Renters don't have it much easier. The vacancy rate in Victoria is 0.5 percent, one of the lowest in the country and rents are increasing at twice the rate of inflation. A survey in 2007 found that over 1,200 people in the capital region are homeless or unsuitably housed. It's not uncommon for families on limited incomes to live in motels in the winter and to camp in the summer. While it's not funny, the price of real estate has inspired some memorable cartoons, such as one by Raeside in the Victoria Times Colonist that depicted real estate posters showing a dog house for $350,000 and a starter tarp going for $179,000.

RENTING

Average monthly rent paid for a 2-bedroom apartment (2006):

• Toronto	$1,067
• Vancouver	$1,045
• Ottawa	$941
• Victoria	$874
• Halifax	$799
• Winnipeg	$709
• Montreal	$636

Take 5 **FIVE BIG ISLANDER**
SALARIES

1. **Steve Nash**, Guard, Phoenix Suns: $10,500,000
2. **Dr. Patrick James McAllister**, Orthopedic Surgeon, Victoria: $662,971
3. **J. William Freytag**, Chairman and CEO, Aspreva Pharmaceuticals Corp., Victoria: $658,500
4. **Raymond Hert**, President and CEO, Western Forest Products Inc.: $400,000
5. **Gordon Campbell**, Premier of British Columbia: $186,200

Average vacancy rate:
- Halifax — 3.2 percent
- Toronto — 3.2 percent
- Montreal — 2.7 percent
- Ottawa — 2.3 percent
- Winnipeg — 1.3 percent
- Vancouver — 0.7 percent
- Victoria — 0.5 percent

Source: Canada Mortgage and Housing Corporation.

They Said It

"It will be a sorry day . . . (for) British Columbians when the forest industry here consists chiefly of a few very big companies, holding most of the good timber—or pretty near all of it—and good growing sites to the disadvantage of the most hard working, virile, versatile and ingenious element of our population, the independent logger and the small mill man."

– H.R MacMillan, in testimony before the 1956 Royal Commission on Forest Resources.

POVERTY

Proportion of recipients of Basic Income Assistance and Employment Insurance in the total population of Vancouver Island ages 19-64:

- June 2007: 3.4 percent
- June 2006: 3.7 percent

HOMELESSNESS

Estimates of minimum numbers of homeless people in Vancouver Island communities by front-line workers in a province-wide survey, November 2007:

British Columbia	10,580
Victoria	1,550
Nanaimo	225
Comox Valley	200
Cowichan Valley and Duncan	200
Port Alberni	112
Port Hardy and Port McNeill	75
Campbell River	35
Salt Spring Island	23
Parksville and Qualicum Beach	10

Sources: Finding Our Way Home: A Consultation on the Homelessness Crisis in BC and BC Statistics.

EMPLOYMENT

- Employment rate (percentage of the population holding a job Vancouver Island/Coast, January 2008): 60.7 percent
- Unemployment rate: 4.5 percent
- Unemployment rate in BC: 4.1 percent
- Unemployment rate in Canada: 6.0 percent

Sources: BC Statistics and Statistics Canada.

Timber Baron

For more than half a century, Harvey Reginald MacMillan's name was virtually synonymous with forestry on Vancouver Island. A bushy-eyebrowed Ontarian with a Master's degree in Forestry from Yale, MacMillan (1885-1976) was just 26 when he was hired as BC's first Chief Forester.

He was much too ambitious to settle in for life in a government job. He soon resigned to go into the lumbering business in Chemainus. He quit that job as well with a now legendary vow: "The next time I walk through this door, Mr. Humbird, I am going to own this mill" — and by 1944 he did.

During a stint with the Imperial Munitions Board during WWI, MacMillan cruised the west coast looking for Sitka spruce. Old-growth spruce had a combination of strength and lightness suitable for making frames for the fighter-planes of the day. After the war, he formed the H.R. MacMillan Export Company to market Douglas fir to overseas markets.

MacMillan saw that owning both the raw material and the means of production was vital to success in the cut-throat, low-margin business of lumbering. During the Depression, he began buying sawmills and private timber. Through mergers and acquisitions, MacMillan built one of the most vertically-integrated forest companies in the world. "HR" built an empire, that at one time produced 25 percent of the lumber on the BC coast and 38 percent of the market pulp. The heart of MacMillan's empire was some of the best coniferous forestland on southeastern Vancouver Island.

It can't be said that HR was an Islander. Although his family maintained a summer cottage in Qualicum Beach, they began living in Vancouver in 1917. HR's name is memorialized in MacMillan Provincial Park near Port Alberni, protecting a forest of old-growth Douglas fir that he donated. But his name disappeared from the annals of business in 1999, when Weyerhaeuser Canada absorbed of MacMillan Bloedel Ltd. Brascan Corp (now Brookfield) bought HR's private forestlands in 2005, and they became the basis of Island Timberlands LLC.

EMPLOYMENT BY SECTOR (PERCENTAGE OF ALL WORKERS)

Total Average Employment, Vancouver Island/Coast, 2007: 378.3 thousand

- Retail/Wholesale Trade: 17.4
- Health Care and Social Assistance: 14.0
- Construction: 9.5
- Accommodation and Food Services: 8.4
- Educational Services: 6.8
- Public Administration: 6.6
- Finance, Insurance, Real Estate and Leasing: 6.1
- Professional, Scientific and Technical Services: 5.8

Take 5 MAJOR PROJECTS UNDERWAY ON VANCOUVER ISLAND

1. **Bear Mountain, Langford** — $1.2 billion. LGB9 Development Corp. is building 2,900 units of single-family homes and condominiums, hotels, 2 golf courses, clubhouse and retail village, for completion in 2014.

2. **Dockside Green, Victoria** — $600 million. Victoria and Windmill West are developing a 6 ha. waterfront site into 1,000 housing units, with office and commercial space and hotel, for completion in 2016.

3. **Bayview, Victoria** — $400 million. Bayview Properties is building 597 units in 3 residential towers and townhouses on Victoria Harbour, for completion in 2010.

4. **Aquattro, Colwood** — $350 million. Ridley Brothers Development Corp. is building 563 units (3 towers, townhouses and condominiums) on a 19-ha. site on Esquimalt Lagoon, for completion in 2012.

5. **NEPTUNE Canada, Victoria** — $300 million. The University of Victoria is laying a 3,000 km network of powered fibre optic cable over the Juan de Fuca tectonic plate as a seafloor observatory, to be completed in 2008.

Take 5 LARGEST COMPANIES
HEADQUARTERED ON VANCOUVER ISLAND

Ranked by 2006 revenue, with rank in the *BC Business* Top One Hundred

1. **Western Forest Products Inc.**, Duncan: $896.8 million, #36
2. **Thrifty Foods Inc.**, Victoria: $552 million, #47
3. **Black Press Ltd.**, Victoria: $390 million, #59
4. **Coast Capital Savings Credit Union**, Victoria: $267 million, #80
5. **Aspreva Pharmaceuticals Corp.**, Victoria: $243 million, #87

Source: BC Business Magazine.

- Manufacturing: 5.1
- Information, Culture and Recreation: 4.5
- Business, Building and other Support Services: 4.3
- Transportation and Warehousing: 4.1
- Other services: 3.4
- Forestry, Fishing, Mining, Oil and Gas: 2.5
- Agriculture: 1.0
- Utilities: 0.5

Source: BC Statistics.

Did you know...

that the BC Forest Discovery Centre has a collection of geared logging "locies" — steam locomotives with gears for climbing steep slopes — and includes three Shay and two Climax locies? The Hillcrest Lumber Company No. 9, built in 1915, is the only operational Climax in the world. They transported logs on Vancouver Island until the 1940s.

GENDER GAP

Women earn approximately 62.8 percent of men's earnings in British Columbia.

Employment rate, March 2008

- BC men 25+ years: 70.6 percent
- BC women 25+ years: 57.7 percent

Percentage employed part-time

- BC men, 25+ years: 7.4 percent
- BC women, 25+ years: 25.8 percent

Source: Statistics Canada.

AbeBooks: Homegrown High-Tech

The world's largest book marketplace started quietly as an off-shoot from a Victoria used bookstore in 1995. The founders, two couples (Rick and Vivian Pura and Keith and Cathy Waters), incorporated and started a website called Advance Book Exchange, developing their own searchable database of the inventories of local booksellers. With that, they started a small revolution in book selling.

By the end of its first year it had two million listings. Today the company lists 110 million books for 13,500 booksellers, mostly independent. In 2007 it sold $190 million (US) worth of books. It has more than 120 employees with offices in Düsseldorf, Germany; Oviedo, Spain; and Berkeley, California; as well as Canada. *Macleans* has named AbeBooks one of Canada's top 100 employers for the past five years.

SMALL BUSINESS (LESS THAN 50 EMPLOYEES)

- Total number of small business establishments on Vancouver Island (2007): 55,744
- Proportion of total business establishments: 98.1 percent
- Average annual growth in number of small business establishments, 2001-2006: 1,600
- Average annual growth rate: 2.8 percent

Sources: Statistics Canada and BC Statistics.

BANKRUPTCIES (2007)

	Consumer	vs 2006	Business	vs 2006
Victoria	640	+9.6 percent	32	−10.3 percent
Nanaimo	202	−0.1 percent	5	−37.5 percent
BC	6,651	−5.3 percent	470	−5.3 percent

Source: BC Statistics.

SELF-EMPLOYMENT

Self-employed workers in BC as of March 2008: 410,900
Proportion of total employed workforce: 17.7 percent

Source: Statistics Canada.

Take 5 **LARGEST EMPLOYERS**
IN THE CAPITAL REGIONAL DISTRICT
(FULL- & PART-TIME WORKERS)

1. **BC Government:** 11,851
2. **Vancouver Island Health Authority:** 6,718
3. **CFB Esquimalt, Department of National Defence:** 6,500
4. **University of Victoria:** 5,319
5. **Victoria School District:** 2,312

Source: Capital Regional District.

Take 5 GUY DAUNCEY'S PLACES

WHERE SUSTAINABILITY IS PRACTISED

Guy Dauncey is widely respected for his tireless and effective work promoting sustainable economies on Vancouver Island. Through his many books and the monthly magazine *EcoNews*, the BC Sustainable Energy Association and other initiatives, he has contributed greatly to the debate and life on the island. Unlike many advocates of change, he emphasizes positive attitude over weight of criticism.

1. **Dockside Green, Victoria**. Dockside Green is one of the greenest large-scale developments in North America, and the first to be fully carbon-neutral from a building perspective. The 6-ha. project on Victoria Harbour is designed to become a thriving human community and a showcase for environmental technologies and building practices.

2. **Salt Spring Seeds, Salt Spring Island**. Dan Jason started Salt Spring Seeds in 1987 to supply the market for organic, untreated, open-pollinated, non-GM seeds gathered from 10 gardens and farms. Dan shares in a larger vision, the Salt Spring Seed Sanctuary, which keeps a living stock of heritage organic seeds for future generations.

3. **Ann and Gord Baird's cob home, Highlands**. These eco-visionaries have built a pioneering almost-zero-energy house for their three-generation family. It is North America's first passive solar, seismically-engineered, load-bearing, insulated cob house, featuring solar photovoltaic and wind power, solar thermal heating, rainwater harvesting from a living roof, a composting toilet and grey water re-use.

4. **Wildwood Forest, near Ladysmith**. Merv Wilkinson is a living legend for applying the best principles of ecosystem management to his 31 ha. private forest. Merv logged Wildwood for top-quality timber beginning in 1945. The standing volume has actually increased, while maintaining all the characteristics of an old-growth forest. The forest was purchased recently and is now operated by the Land Conservancy of BC, with tours every Saturday at 1:30 pm.

5. **Clayoquot Sound**. Clayoquot Sound is an amazing wildscape of ancient temperate forests and abundant forest and marine life. It was designated a Biosphere Reserve by UNESCO in recognition of its global cultural and ecological importance. The Friends of Clayoquot Sound, based in Tofino, are committed to preserving the wildness and beauty of the region.

BUILDING PERMITS
Vancouver Island/Coast, 2007

	$ MILLION	VS 2006
Residential	1,316.8	+7.3 percent
Institutional/Government	266.0	+64.9 percent
Commercial	229.9	−18.4 percent
Industrial	30.1	−2.2 percent

High Tech

Southeast Vancouver Island is now a fast-growing high-technology centre, with more than 1,200 companies. A high percentage of the companies are home-grown, including Aspreva Pharmaceuticals and other biomedical companies. Custom House is the largest non-bank foreign exchange company in North America and one of the largest in the world, and robotics manufacturer Triton Logging makes chainsaws that log forests submerged under dam reservoirs – the ultimate in green high-tech.

The sector employs an estimated 17,000 workers on the island, including many highly trained scientists, technologists and engineers. Total revenues for fiscal 2006/07 were estimated at $2.4 billion. Assisting its growth is the University of Victoria-hosted Innovation and Development Corp. UVic also operates the Vancouver Island Technology Park.

HIGH TECH COMPANIES ON VANCOUVER ISLAND
ESTIMATED EMPLOYMENT AND REVENUE, 2007:

	# OF COMPANIES	# OF EMPLOYEES	REVENUE (2006/07)
Greater Victoria	878	12,700	$1,700 m
Mid-Island	324	4,600	$670 m
Total	1,202	17,300	$2,370 m

Source: BC Regional Science and Technology Network.

Value of building permits in selected cities, February 2008:

	$ MILLION
Victoria	74.3
Vancouver	447.5
Calgary	605.9
Toronto	881.8
Ottawa	118.0
Montreal	497.6

Sources: Statistics Canada and BC Statistics.

PASSENGER VOLUME AT REGIONAL AIRPORTS (2007)

Victoria	1,481,606
Comox	310,175
Nanaimo	139,449
Campbell River	61,080

Source: Tourism British Columbia.

ANNUAL TRAFFIC THROUGH VANCOUVER ISLAND PORTS
Tonnes of Cargo

Campbell River	1,000,000
Crofton	800,000
Nanaimo	616,000
Port Alberni	100,000

Sources: Government of BC.

Did you know...

that rockfish often live in excess of 150 years and are sometimes called "scorpionfish" because of their spiney, venom-filled dorsal fins? Their defenses have not prevented BC's 34 species of rockfish from being dangerously overfished. Canada has now established more than 160 Rockfish Conservation Areas in BC.

BIGGEST FERRY ROUTES,
VANCOUVER ISLAND (2006/07):

	PASSENGERS	VEHICLES
1. **Swartz Bay-Tsawwassen**	6.1 million	1.9 million
2. **Departure Bay–Horseshoe Bay**	3.7	1.3
3. **Duke Point-Tsawwassen**	1.4	0.6
4. **Campbell River-Quadra Island**	0.91	0.42
5. **Nanaimo Harbour-Gabriola Island**	0.87	0.40

Source: BC Ferries.

BC FERRIES

BC Ferries, the coastal ferry system, is rightly called a marine highway. For travel and transport between the islands and with the mainland, it provides essential services. From two vessels in 1960, BC Ferries' fleet has grown to 37. They make 188,000 trips a year, with a staff of 4,700 during the busy summer months. Of BC Ferries' 25 routes, 18 serve Vancouver Island, including the three major ones.

- Total number of vehicles carried (2006/07): 8.5 million
- Total number of passengers carried: 21.7 million
- Revenues (2006/07): $596.3 million
- 1995 fare for car and driver, Swartz Bay-Tsawwassen: $26.75
- 2008 fare for same: $56.
- Increase: 108 percent, or 8.3 percent/year.

Source: Victoria Times-Colonist.

Did you know...

that Greater Victoria has 4,340 hotel rooms?

MINES AND QUARRIES OPERATING ON VANCOUVER ISLAND

- Myra Falls: metal mine (zinc, copper, gold, silver) near Campbell River
- Quinsam: thermal coal mine near Campbell River
- Apple Bay: chalky geyserite quarry
- Benson Lake: limestone quarry

Source: Ministry of Energy, Mines and Petroleum Resources.

ENERGY

Two-thirds of Vancouver Island's electricity comes in two sets of underwater cables across the Strait of Georgia. Most of the rest is from hydroelectric generators and a natural gas/diesel cogeneration plant at the Elk Falls pulp and paper mill. The total supply, some 2,300 megawatts (MW), is barely able to meet peak usage and will not satisfy the island's growing energy budget. BC Hydro projects the load is expected to

Did you know...

that tyee fishing, a Campbell River institution, involves pairs of fishers rowing the pools of Discovery Passage in search of Chinook salmon? One rows, the other trolls. Wrestle a 30-pounder into the boat on 20-pound line and you're a member of the Tyee Club (founded 1925). The 2007 record catch was 42 pounds.

increase from 1.1 percent to 1.7 percent over the next two decades. Twin natural gas pipelines have supplied Vancouver Island since 1991.

Finding new and clean sources of energy supply has developed a sense of urgency on the island since a planned natural gas-burning plant at Duke Point and a new pipeline from the mainland were shelved in 2005.

"Run-of-river" (no dam) hydroelectric projects sell power to BC Hydro. As of April 2008, seven generators are operating on the island. They contribute about two percent of its overall energy supply. Dozens more are in development. The run-of-river program is controversial because of the impact on other resources and such industries as river-based recreation, and concerns about the cost of energy.

Other small developments include a cogeneration plant at Victoria's Hartland landfill that burns methane gas to generate 1.6 MW. A project to use the abandoned Gold River pulp mill to generate electricity by burning garbage is in the planning stage. A small tidal generator is operating in Race Rocks Ecological Reserve in an experiment run by Lester B. Pearson College of the Pacific.

FORESTRY

Since the early 1990's, BC's coastal timber industry has largely stagnated. Rising costs, slumping demand for dimension lumber and the strong Canadian dollar have taken heavy tolls on earnings. Today, forestry's share of GDP has declined to just over seven percent, and less than 15 with indirect and induced value-added.

By the Numbers — GDP Attributable to BC Forest Industries

- Forestry and logging: $3,272 million
- Wood product manufacturing: $4,902 million
- Pulp and paper manufacturing: $1,404 million
- Pulp, paper and paperboard mills: $1,280 million
- Converted paper product manufacturing: $124 million
- Total: $10,982 million
- Total BC GDP: $146,284 million

THE FORESTLAND PIE

A whopping 19,000 km^2 or 55 percent of Vancouver Island is public forest land, and more than 18 percent is private. (A high proportion of Vancouver Island is privately-owned. In all BC, just 5 percent is private.) Overall, 80 percent of the island is dedicated to forestry.

Public forestland is owned by the province and allocated to timber companies in several kinds of licences. The major kind is called a tree farm licence (TFL), which gives a company exclusive logging rights and management duties to an area. One company now manages 12,000 km^2 in six TFLs on the island. The total allowable annual cut in TFLs is 7 million m^3/year, and Western Forest Products Ltd. has 83 percent of it.

Companies with private holdings are TimberWest Corp. — the island's largest landowner, with 3,340 km^2 — and Island Timberlands LC with 2,580 km^2.

Sources: Ministry of Forests, TimberWest, Island Timberlands.

THE LITTLE PULP MILL THAT COULD

The antique Port Alice dissolving sulphite pulp mill produces many specialty cellulose products like rayon for which there is steady demand and few competitors. The village of Port Alice weathered the previous owner's bankruptcy and 18-month closure in 2004 before the mill started up again, under the management of Neucel Speciality Cellulose Ltd. Neucal is controlled by Wellspring Capital Management (New York) and CSG Group (New Jersey).

FISHERIES / AQUACULTURE

The commercial fisheries, once an economic mainstay of coastal BC, have shrunk significantly. Sport fishery (a service industry interrelated with tourism) is holding its own, however, and wild salmon stocks still provide thousands of Vancouver Islanders with revenue and employment. Meanwhile, open-pen salmon farming has grown into a sizeable industry, especially on the northeast quarter of the island, but many view them as a threat to wild salmon stocks. Aquaculture, salt-water farming of both fish and shellfish, contributes nearly $800 million to BC's GDP, 0.6 percent of the total.

GDP of BC Fisheries and Aquaculture Industries, 1984 vs 2005:

	1984	2005	Percent change
Aquaculture	$3 million	$274 million	+9,000
Sport fishing	$253 million	$248 million	−2.1
Fish processing	$172 million	$173 million	+0.8
Commercial fishery	$148 million	$103 million	−30.2

BC's Commercial Fishery Revenues, 2005:

Groundfish	$29 million
Halibut	$17 million
Geoducks and clams	$14 million
Herring	$8 million
Salmon	$6 million
Other	$27 million
Total	$103 million

Economic Impacts of BC's Salmon Fisheries, 2005:

- Direct output (sales/service): $818 million
- Employment (full-time-equivalent): 5,380
- Alaska-caught salmon accounted for about half the value of salmon canned in BC in 2005 and is included in employment figure.

Source: BC Statistics and Legislative Assembly of BC.

TOURISM

Tourism has become one of the island's staple industries. Tourism includes a broad spectrum of services from premier hotels and amenities to mom-and-pop retailers. Tourism marketing emphasizes the island's natural beauty, healthy environment and built heritage. Province-wide, it accounts for 4 percent of GDP and employs more than 120,000 people, full-time and part-time. Every indicator shows steady growth.

TOURISM GDP

BC GDP attributable to tourism, 2006: $5.49 billion

Change from previous year: +4.6 percent

- Transportation and related: $1,993 million (+3.6 percent)
- Accommodation & food services: $1,935 million (+5.7 percent)
- Other tourism services: $997 million (+3.5 percent)
- Tourism retailing: $565 million (+6.0 percent)

Source: BC Statistics.

Whale Watching

When BC's first whale watching enterprise was established in 1980, orcas were still called killer whales and routinely shot. Statistics on the growth of the industry are scarce, but some 60 whale-watching operators and facilitators operate on Vancouver Island. A third of them are on the west coast, a third on the east coast, and a third around Victoria.

The whale-watching season begins in early spring when the gray whales arrive. One of the best areas for orca watching is Broughton Archipelago, off the northeast coast, where both resident and transient pods converge. The Robson Bight (Michael Bigg) Ecological Reserve protects the vicinity of an orca rubbing beach.

Weblinks

Business Vancouver Island

Online news clearinghouse that is the voice for local businesses.
http://www.businessvi.ca/

Business Examiner

Business and general news source for Vancouver Island that allows you to search by region.
http://www.bclocalnews.com/businessexaminer/vancouver_island/

Business Vancouver Island

A free, high-quality search engine to help you find business directory listings all over Vancouver Island.
http://www.businessvancouverisland.com/

Crime and Punishment

CRIMELINE

1851: Early policing on Vancouver Island consists of a volunteer force known as the Victoria Voltigeurs.

1853: The first trial is held in the colony of Vancouver Island. Two First Nations men are found guilty in the murder of Peter Brown. They are executed at Gallows Point on Protection Island. M. Rowland, the executioner at Nanaimo, was paid six pounds, 17 shillings and sixpence for his services.

1858: Augustus Pemberton is appointed the first commissioner of the Victoria Metropolitan Police.

1859: Constable Johnston Cochrane is shot and killed under mysterious circumstances. He becomes the first officer in Victoria to lose his life in the line of duty.

1860: The Victoria Police Department is formed. Chief Francis O'Conner is responsible for supervising 12 constables, a sanitary officer, a night watchman and a jailer.

1866: The police forces on Vancouver Island and the mainland are amalgamated into the British Columbia Constabulary (BCC).

1867-68: William Robinson (a Black man) is brutally murdered on Salt Spring Island. One First Nations man, Tshuanahusset, is arrested, convicted and hanged for Robinson's murder — many believe wrongly. What makes the case suspicious is that shortly after Robinson's murder and Tshuanahusset's conviction another Black man is murdered. Police also say the murder weapon was lost after it fell out of a canoe.

1870: Twenty-two BCC officers are responsible for patrolling 250,000 square miles in British Columbia. The population at that time includes 5,782 white men, 2,794 white women, 297 black men, 165 black women, 1,495 Chinese men, 53 Chinese women and approximately 26,000 First Nations people.

1871: The combined island and mainland force is given the new name of the British Columbia Provincial Police.

Chinook Jargon

In the early years of British Columbia, Chinook Jargon was the standard form of communication between the Colony of Vancouver Island government and First Nations peoples. The jargon was based on the pre-contact trade language of First Nations groups in the area, with a few French and English words thrown in.

While it was used in all legal capacities – from treaty signing to murder trials — the language had its limitations. It was simplistic and ambiguous and had a vocabulary that never exceeded 800 words. In court, the language gap proved devastating for First Nations people, many of whom often had no way of understanding the charges against them.

KAY STEWART'S TOP FIVE
REASONS VANCOUVER ISLAND IS SUCH A GREAT PLACE TO WRITE CRIME NOVELS

Kay Stewart taught English for many years at the University of Alberta before turning her attention to writing crime fiction. She is an active member of Crime Writers of Canada. Salt Spring Island provides the setting for her first novel, *A Deadly Little List*. Her new novel *Sitting Lady Sutra* involves a serial killer in the Victoria area.

1. **Funky communities.** The incident that suggested the plot of *A Deadly Little List* occurred in Alberta, but the novel didn't come alive until we decided to set it on Salt Spring, with its overlapping communities of artists, craftspeople, hippies, environmentalists, and wealthy developers.

2. **Rich history.** Crimes grow out of specific historical and cultural conditions. Many events in the diverse history of Vancouver Island and the Gulf Islands, such as the abuse of First Nations children in residential schools and the internment of coastal Japanese immigrants during World War II, have had long-lasting consequences that influence the characters I write about.

3. **Intriguing places.** Sitting Lady Falls in Witty's Lagoon Regional Park, Metchosin, becomes a dominant image in my current novel, *Sitting Lady Sutra*. The Hell's Angel clubhouse in Nanaimo (recently shut down by the RCMP) also intrigues me.

4. **Fascinating events.** Every year, members of the RCMP cycle from one end of Vancouver Island to the other to raise money for cancer research. I'm itching to make this event central to a novel.

5. **Alternative approaches to criminal justice.** The Victoria area is home not only to the Island Headquarters of the RCMP but also to William Head Institution (formerly a medium security federal prison, now minimum), with its stage productions, restorative justice program, and other initiatives that build bridges between those on the inside and those on the outside and remind us of our common humanity.

Rum Running

Prohibition in British Columbia began at the end of WWI and ended in 1920. In neighbouring Washington state, it came into effect in 1916 and in the rest of the US in 1920. Prohibition in the US lasted until 1933, when the 18th Amendment was repealed.

From 1920-1933 rum running was a quasi-legal and thriving business venture on the island. The attraction for many Islanders was that it paid much better than the fishing trade. The new industry also suited an island penchant for adventure. Unlike the mafia run East Coast business, the Pacific rum running trade was smaller and largely free of big gang influence.

One well-known smuggler, Lieutenant (Whiskers) William Lowell Thompson. Thompson typified the type of enterprise on the Island. Thompson came to Vancouver Island in 1896, settling in Ucluelet where he made a typical New World living working as a general merchant, farmer and fisherman as well as prospecting. Before long he had established himself as an imprtant member of the community.

With the onsent of WWI, Thompson found that his considerable skills on the water were very much in short supply. He enlisted, becoming a First Lietennant in the Royal Navy. Thompson would not be demobilized until 1919. He returned to Ucluelet but a post-war recession and a new found sense of adventure were not quite enough for Thompson.

With the passing of the Volstead Act (Prohibition) in 1920, it was the beginning of a whole new industry in Canada, and tailor made for an ambitious man like Thompson. He quickly moved to Victoria, operating a range of vessels under various guises of legitimate enterprises. In one instance he was caught off the coast of California but managed to escape in the dead of night, his cargo still intact.

Thompson had obviously made his fortune in liquor trade, but after the repeal of the Volstead Act what Thompson hadn't lost was his sense of adventure. In 1930, Thompson was registered as the president of the company that bought the 259-ton, oil-fired steamer, the *Chasina*.

In 1931, the *Chasina* departed Victoria for Shanghai. There are no documents, of course, but speculation is that the *Chasina* was seeking to either import opium or illegal Chinese workers into North America. There are records of the *Chasina* leaving Macao, but the vessel and Thompson would never be seen again.

1905: Victoria Police Department gets their first horse-drawn patrol wagon.

1906: Oak Bay and Saanich get their own police departments. Oak Bay's only police officer is provided with an 8x10-foot room built within the municipal stable. It serves double duty as his headquarters and home. The community of Saanich provides Constable Jabez Russell with a horse.

Judge Begbie

Matthew Baillie Begbie arrived at Fort Victoria in 1858 at the age of 39 after a successful law practice in London, England. Why? He loved travel and adventure. He first served as a Judge of the Supreme Court for the colony of British Columbia, then in the same capacity for the United Colonies of Vancouver Island and BC. His imposing size (6'5") and nerve helped the colony's first judge on the mining frontier. Governor James Douglas was looking for a man who could bring law and order to the rough and tumble colony and who could "if necessary, truss a murderer up and hang him from the nearest tree."

Begbie is remembered as the Hanging Judge. A wag suggested he was more properly the Haranguing Judge because of the lectures he gave from the bench. Of the 52 murder cases he heard, one-half ended in hangings. Hanging was mandatory for murder convictions. When not riding the circuit, Begbie lived in Victoria. A lifelong bachelor and man of culture, he was (among many offices) the first president of the Victoria Philharmonic Society.

In 1871, Begbie became the first Chief Justice of the Supreme Court of BC, a post he held until his death in 1894. Queen Victoria knighted him in 1875. Some claim the Hanging Judge still walks the corridors of the old Provincial Court House in Victoria.

They Said It

> "If these cases are allowed to continue with impunity there is no knowing where they will end. The mere fact of there being a Constable at the Lake would be sufficient to stop many of these depredations."
>
> – In a Lake Cowichan newspaper in 1915 in response to the trial of two men who were charged with hunting one hour after sunset.

1907: A newspaper article states that William Clarke Quantrill, a notorious and vicious outlaw from the American Civil War, is living in Quatsino under the alias John Sharp. Sharp is mysteriously murdered shortly after the story runs in US newspapers.

1908: The Opium Act is the first federal law in North America to outlaw drugs.

1913: Troops are dispatched to Nanaimo and Ladysmith to stop rioting between striking mine workers and strikebreakers.

1915: Robert Suttie becomes the last person to be hanged on Vancouver Island. After 1919, all executions are carried out at Oakalla Prison in Burnaby. Suttie is convicted for the murder of Richard Hargreaves.

Did you know...

that in the early 1900's complaints for the police often arrived by mail?

Did you know...

that 68-year-old Francis Rattenbury, the architect of the British Columbia Parliament Buildings, was murdered in England by his second wife's 18-year-old lover?

1915: Anti-German rioting takes place in Victoria after the sinking of the British luxury ocean liner *Lusitania*, off the coast of Ireland.

1918: Victoria Police get their first motorized patrol wagon.

1918: Union organizer Albert "Ginger" Goodwin is shot by Dominion Police Special Constable Dan Campbell outside Cumberland. His murder sparks Canada's first general strike.

The Poet and the Bandit

Susan Musgrave grew up on Vancouver Island and published her first book of poems, *Songs of the Sea Witch*, when she was just 19. Almost four decades later, Susan Musgrave is an author of national stature.

In 1975, she married criminal lawyer Jeffrey Green, but the marriage lasted only four years. When Green was acting for a group of accused marijuana smugglers, Musgrave fell for one of the accused, Paul Nelson. When Nelson was acquitted, Musgrave went with him to Mexico. Together, they had a daughter. When Nelson was later convicted on an old smuggling charge in California and found religion, the marriage came to an abrupt end.

Musgrave received a manuscript from convicted bank robber, Stephen Reid, who was serving a twenty-year sentence at Millhaven Penitentiary in Ontario. It was the manuscript for the memoir *Jackrabbit Parole*, the chronicle of his career with the Stopwatch Gang. She fell in love and married the author while he was still in prison. The book was published the same year. When Reid was released from prison the following year he and Musgrave moved to Vancouver Island where they had a daughter together. Reid continued to write while succumbing to a lifelong addiction to hard drugs.

On June 9, 1999, Reid, dressed as a police officer and carrying a sawed-off shotgun, robbed a bank in Victoria. Fleeing with $92,924 in a getaway car, he hung out the passenger window, shooting at pursuing police. Ironically, the couple was the subject of a CBC documentary that aired the same year called "The Poet and the Bandit." Reid was sentenced to eighteen years in prison. He was released on day parole in January 2008.

Take 5 MICHAEL HALLERAN'S FIVE
GRAVES TO VISIT AT ROSS BAY CEMETERY

Ross Bay Cemetery in Victoria is the final resting place of many notable Islanders, including James Douglas, BC's first governor; coal baron Robert Dunsmuir; Sir Matthew Baillie Begbie, the Hanging Judge; and Emily Carr. Michael Halleran runs the Murder Most Foul Tours. Not everyone in the Ross Bay Cemetery came to a happy ending. Here are his picks for the five most gruesome graves to visit.

1. **Site P 103 104EU: Cora Maude Anderson and George Anderson.** At 1:00 am on August 22nd, 1915, Cora Maude Anderson, 33, murdered her 48-year-old husband George with an axe as he lay asleep in their bedroom at 35 Lewis Street in James Bay. When she completed the task, she laid the axe on the blood soaked bed, shut the door, and blocked the entryway by pulling a bureau in front of it. Cora then put on her hat and coat, walked out, locked the front door and promptly headed for Holland Point where she drowned herself.

2. **Site O81 EL: William Tyrill.** William Tyrill was one of the miners who discovered gold at Leechtown in 1864. Gold, however, is not what brought about his death. William Tyrill died as a result of a triangle of jealousy, seasoned with a good dollop of racism. The centre of the triangle was a widow named Mrs. Cargill. Mrs. Cargill was friends with Tyrill but was also seeing a stoker named Donald McKay from the steamer *Otter*. McKay disapproved of her friendship with Tyrill both because he was jealous and because Tyrill was black. On April 19th, 1907, McKay beat Tyrill to death.

3. **Site B84 W36: Charlie Kincaid.** On Friday, June 3, 1898, pimp Charles Kincaid lay dead on the sidewalk in front of the Empire Hotel at 546 Johnson Street, his throat slit open with a razor by Bella Adams, one of his prostitutes and lovers. Charlie and Bella had an

abusive relationship, punctuated by violence. Things came to a boil the day before the murder. Bella heard that Charlie was going to leave her and go off to Vancouver with another woman, so when the time was ripe Bella grabbed Charlie's razor and slashed him. Clutching his throat, Charlie staggered from the room, down the stairs, out the door where he fell on the sidewalk moaning, "She's killed me, my God, she's killed me." Bella was put on trial for murder. The defense made much of the abusive nature of her relationship with Charlie. She was convicted of the lesser charge of manslaughter and sentenced to five years in the Penitentiary for Women in Kingston, Ontario.

4. **Site A48E: Henry Forman.** City of Victoria Alderman Henry Forman was shot January 22, 1874. He was eating dinner peacefully at home with his wife, daughter and infant granddaughter when his son-in-law, Thomas Schooley, came through the door and killed him. Forman had taken his daughter and grandchild into his house after Schooley had become abusive toward them. Schooley was later convicted of murder and hanged.

5. **Site N42 EQ: William Millington.** Few murderers are buried in Ross Bay Cemetery. Tradition was that if you were convicted in a court of law and hanged a murderer you would be buried in an unmarked grave on the grounds of the gaol. William Millington, however, is the exception to this rule. He was a murderer who was acquitted. Millington shot Robert Coombs, a 30-year-old sailor from the *H.M.S. Plumper*. The jury found Millington innocent, ruling self-defense. The newspapers would point out later that the innocent verdict was more a reflection of prejudice against Armed Forces personnel than a reflection of truth.

1950: The British Columbia Provincial Police is absorbed into the RCMP.

1958: BC forests minister Robert Sommers is sentenced to five years in jail for bribery and conspiracy, making him the first Cabinet minister to serve time in the British Commonwealth.

1977: 12-year-old Carolyn Lee is abducted and murdered in Port Alberni. As a result of her death, the Block Parent program is introduced into Port Alberni.

1979: More than 33.5 tonnes of Columbian marijuana is seized from the vessel *Samarkanda* in Sydney Inlet near Tofino. All aboard are acquitted of drug smuggling when they raise the defense of necessity, saying they didn't intend to import drugs into Canada but were simply offloading the marijuana because they were hung up on a reef and in danger of capsizing.

Criminal Theatrics

William Head Penitentiary in Metchosin is home to a unique theatrical troop. William Head on Stage (WHoS) is an inmate-operated theatre that has been performing plays for the public for the past 26 years. From Shakespeare's Macbeth to One Flew Over the Cuckoo's Nest, the prisoner's theatre board chooses the play (with approval from the administration) then hires the director.

Then the troop rehearses and prepares for opening night. WhoS has a few issues that are unique to prison theatre — actors need to be chosen on the basis of availability (parole, transfers and releases need to be covered by understudies) and the audience needs to be let in and out of the prison's gates for each performance.

They Said It

"When horrid tragedies are being enacted so near to our homes in such rapid succession, it is no time for indolence on the part of the Government. We ask, on behalf of the public, for information."

– From a report in the *British Colonist* on January 4, 1869. The concern is over the unsolved murders of three black men on Salt Spring Island.

1991: Five-year-old Michael Dunahee is abducted just metres away from his parents at a playground; there are no witnesses. The case results in one of the largest investigations in Canadian history, but Michael has never been found.

1997: Reena Virk, 14, of Saanich is swarmed and beaten by a group of teenagers. Two of the attackers then dump her and leave her to drown in Victoria's Gorge waterway. Six girls are found guilty of assault. Seventeen-year-old Warren Glowatski and Kelly Ellard, 15, are found guilty of second-degree murder. Ellard won an appeal that overturned her conviction, and her second trial resulted in a hung jury; a third trial sentenced her to life imprisonment, but Ellard has appealed the case, and the Virk family faces the possibility of having to endure a fourth murder trial. Ellard has never admitted responsibility for Reena's death.

Victoria Voltigeurs

Vancouver Island's first armed militia style force became known as the Victoria Voltigeurs. Hand-picked by Governor James Douglas, this small, mobile infantry numbered between six and thirty was largely made up of a group of mixed-race men. They included various Kanaka (Pacific Islanders), Black and Metis. Being of mixed-race himself, Douglas proudly referred to his militia men as 'half-white.' The Victoria Voltigeurs disbanded in 1858, when the gold rush brought an influx of white Europeans who refused to be policed by a non-English force.

1998: Nine people are arrested in a drug bust at the dock at Fanny Bay. Twelve metric tonnes of hashish worth an estimated $46 million is seized. It becomes the largest bust in BC history.

2004: Nine people are convicted in the biggest hashish bust in the province's history (Fanny Bay). The trial is one of the longest in BC provincial court, lasting more than three years and hearing from more than 100 witnesses.

2007: Police raid an alleged Hells Angels clubhouse in downtown Nanaimo and turn it over to the BC government. The Civil Forfeiture Act was passed in May 2006 to allow the province to seize property that was used for unlawful activity.

2008: The fifth severed foot in a year (not including one fake foot) washes ashore between Vancouver and Vancouver Island. To date, only one foot has been identified through DNA.

Did you know...

that prohibition for indigenous peoples lasted from 1854 to 1962? Magistrate Roderick Haig-Brown found the practice unfair and in the late 1950s he said, "It is not simply a question of liquor, but of freedom, and human dignity that belongs with freedom. I am ashamed every time it is the duty of my court to punish Indians for something that is a crime only for them."

Did you know...

that according to a 2006 report by Simon Fraser University, if you look at violent crime, serious property crime and non-cannabis drug crime, the safest place to live in BC is Vancouver Island?

CRIME BY THE NUMBERS

Incidents of crime per 100,000 residents:

	Victoria	BC	Canada
Homicides	1.1	2.5	1.9
Assaults	655.3	979.9	734.8
Robberies	29.8	110.3	94.1
Break and enters	869.1	1,088.3	767.8
Drug violations	353.2	616.8	294.8

Source: Statistics Canada.

IN THE LINE OF DUTY

1859 Const. Johnston Cochrane died by gunfire.

1864 Const. John Curry died by accidental gunfire.

1865 Const. John Ogilvie died by gunfire.

1913 Const. Harry Westaway died by gunfire.

1927 Const. Albert Ernest Wells was killed in a motorcycle accident.

1939 Const. Clifford A. Prescott fell from a cliff.

1941 Const. Frank P. Clark was killed in an automobile accident.

1959 Const. Earle Michael Doyle was killed in a motorcycle accident.

1960 Const. Robert Norman Barry Kirby died by gunfire.

1964 Const. Reginald Wayne Williams drowned.

1971 Const. Michael R. Mason drowned.

1977 Special Const. George David Foster was killed in an aircraft accident.

1980 Auxiliary Const. Dennis Lenard Fraser was killed in an automobile accident.

1983 Corporal Francis Eugene Jones and Special Constable Wayne Graham Myers were killed in an aircraft accident.

1991 Const. Christopher Collin Riglar was struck by a vehicle.

Source: Officer Down Memorial Website.

STOLEN CARS

316 vehicles per 100,000 were stolen in Victoria during 2006. This is better than the national average of 487.2 per 100,000 and well below BC's overall rate of 682.2 vehicles. PEI is the safest place to park your car — only 114.8 cars per 100,000 went missing there. Meanwhile, Manitoba looks like a good place to skip car ownership and invest in a bus pass — a whopping 1,375.7 cars per 100,000 were stolen in the same year.

Source: Statistics Canada.

IMPAIRED DRIVING

Victoria residents have a pretty good record when it comes to drinking and driving, compared to the rest of the country. The rate of impaired driving in Victoria is 153.2 cases per 100,000 residents. Compare this with BC's average of 339.6, Manitoba's of 212.8 and PEI's of 396.6.

Source: Statistics Canada.

FINE, THEN
In Nanaimo:

- Disturbing the peace will cost you $150
- Jay walking is $50
- If your livestock gets free and is found on the highway the penalty will be $50 (poultry is $10)
- Impoundment of a licensed dog is $30
- Impoundment of an unlicensed dog is $100
- Speeding just about anywhere around the city will cost you $100
- Parking on a street beyond the time limit is $30 ($7.50 if paid within 72 hours)
- Failing to stop for a red light will cost you $100

Source: City of Nanaimo Website.

CORRECTIONAL FACILITIES

Vancouver Island has one federal and two provincial facilities.

- Nanaimo Correctional Centre is a minimum security, 170-man facility providing training in substance abuse management, violence prevention and respectful relationships.

- Vancouver Island Regional Correctional Centre, Victoria, has a maximum capacity of 294 men and serves as a remand and sentence facility for all risk levels.
- William Head Penitentiary is a 158-man minimum-security federal facility.

Source: Ministry of Public Safety.

Weblinks

The Officer Down Memorial Page

www.odmp.org/canada/

This website details the deaths of police officers who died in the line of duty.

The RCMP in British Columbia

bc.rcmp.ca

This website tells about "E" Division listing news, detachments and recruitment information.

Victoria Area Policing

www.saanichpolice.ca

www.oakbaypolice.org

www.victoriapolice.org

These three websites give the history and detachment information for Saanich, Oak Bay and Victoria.

Politics

Vancouver Island was once the province's economic engine as well as its political centre. That all changed in 1886 when the first Canadian Pacific Railway train rolled into its western terminus on Burrard Inlet, where the great city of Vancouver would soon develop. By the end of the century, economic power had already shifted to the mainland. Victoria, the provincial capital, remains the centre of political life in BC.

How Victoria became the capital — that's a story with many twists. It begins in 1778, in the era of seagoing European empires.

TRADING PARTNER TO COLONY

In California, Spain had a flourishing colony. In Alaska, Russia had isolated permanent settlements. In between, there was nothing — at least, not on the maps of the day. In fact all along the Pacific coast, First Nations thrived under chiefly forms of government — sovereign local chiefs of Coast Salish peoples; alliances and confederations among Nuu-Chah-Nulth First Nations. With abundant natural resources, the indigenous peoples were seasoned traders, and many were feared as fighters.

In 1778, Captain James Cook happened on Vancouver Island while searching for the fabled Northwest Passage. He would call it Nootka. After Cook's discovery, explorers and traders quickly followed, coming from Spain, England, France and the USA.

A major diplomatic uproar followed. Who owned Nootka? England

They Said It

and Spain, old enemies, squared off. Spain yielded and surveyor Capt. George Vancouver claimed Northwest America for the English sovereign in 1792. England left to American traders the lucrative sea otter business with First Nations. When the animals became extinct from California to Alaska, the American traders left, too.

Into this void chugged the paddle-wheeled trading vessels of the Hudson's Bay Company (HBC). Their maritime base was Fort Vancouver, established 1825 on the Columbia River near present day Portland, Oregon. American settlers in Oregon Country made Fort Vancouver untenable, and chief trader James Douglas proposed moving the base of operation to Quadra's and Vancouver's Island as it was known then.

Tiny Fort Victoria, established 1843, and the HBC colony of Vancouver Island, established 1849, came under Douglas's dual authority of HBC chief and governor of the colony. The British government sent Richard Blanshard, a wet-behind-the-ears barrister, to be governor, but he soon left, and Douglas got himself appointed governor. Only a few hundred settlers braved the passage around Cape Horn. In 1855 a British naval base was established on Esquimalt Harbour. The First Nations population far outnumbered settlers, especially in summer, when upwards of 2,000 people paddled from distant coastal villages to visit Fort Victoria.

Did you know...

that Canada's first Prime Minister, John A. Macdonald was also MP for Victoria during the years 1878-1882? Macdonald never actually lived in Victoria, but when he lost his seat in Kingston, Ontario in the general election of 1878, Victoria was considered a safe Conservative riding.

Bennett's Navy

Over the decades, myriad ferries and other passenger vessels have linked Vancouver Island with Vancouver, Seattle and other nearby ports. The legendary *SS Cassiar* of the Union Steamship line out of Vancouver served the far-flung northeast coast camps. The CPR Coast Steamship Service operated the famous Triangle Route (Victoria-Seattle-Vancouver). Its west coast lifeline, *SS Maquinna*, called in at every port between Victoria and Port Alice.

Seattle-based Puget Sound Navigation Company, the so-called Black Ball Line, competed with the CPR on the US mainland routes for decades. The early ferries were steam-powered, but inevitably, in the 20s, the CPR's *Motor Princess*, the celebrated Galloping Dishpan, started carrying cars on the Nanaimo-Vancouver run.

By 1958, the CPR and Black Ball Ferries Inc. both operated car ferries on several lines between island and mainland, while Washington State Ferries worked the Sidney-Anacortes route. That summer the BC government invited the world to come and celebrate British Columbia's centenary. Vancouver Island promoted tourism heavily.

Before the summer even began, ferry workers started going on strike, having worked with no contract for almost a year. In July they all but shut Vancouver Island off from the world, although the Washington-owned Sidney ferry kept operating.

The federal government refused to use its powers to end the strike. Premier WAC Bennett (Social Credit) vowed that "in the future, ferry connections between Vancouver Island and the Mainland shall not be subject either to the whim of union policy nor to the indifference of federal agencies."

The province bought the five vessels and other assets of Black Ball Ferries and established the BC Ferry Authority. It built the first two ferries at the Victoria Machinery Depot and terminals at Swartz Bay and Tsawwassen. The 35 km service launched on June 15, 1960.

As the fleet grew and grew again, it became known as Bennett's Navy. Today it is arguably the largest ferry fleet in the world.

They Said It

COLONY TO PROVINCE

In 1858, gold was discovered in the river sand of the Fraser Canyon, and within weeks the first wave in a deluge of 20,000-30,000 men, many of them leftover Forty-Niners, were on their way from San Francisco. Fort Victoria was en route. Douglas appointed himself administrator of the gold fields and proclaimed the need to obtain a $5 mining licence at Fort Victoria. The Royal Navy was called in to turn back the scofflaws. Fort Victoria was suddenly crawling with thousands of miners on a shopping spree. It was the first of many booms to hit Vancouver Island.

Overnight, the Gold Rush made the island colony's fortune. The Crown took over the venture and also chartered a new mainland colony, called British Columbia. James Douglas left the HBC to serve as governor of both colonies until retiring in 1864. When the two colonies united in 1866, Victoria lost its status as the capital city to upstart New Westminster.

The HBC cronies made sure Victoria was soon restored as the seat of government. Douglas is often referred to as the founder of British Columbia because, guided by his vision and iron rule, a tiny HBC outpost grew into a vast province of Canada in the space of less than 30 years. In fact, Douglas was always advancing his own and his friends' interests, and he became the richest man on Vancouver Island.

Joining Confederation in 1871 brought parliamentary responsible government to BC, and elected local élites replaced British appointees. But the old boys threw another spanner in the works. Of BC's three negotiators of the terms of union with Canada, two were islanders. One of them, Joseph Trutch, was appointed BC's first lieutenant-governor, prompting Henry Crease to remark, "It's a one-man government still — in disguise."

They Said It

> "You had better not go outside. There is a crowd waiting for you and threaten to be revenged on you."
>
> **– owner of the Colonial Hotel, New Westminster, to Vancouver Island delegates celebrating the vote that restored Victoria as the capital of BC, May 1868. The victorious delegation was led by John Sebastian Helmcken, HBC doctor in Victoria and son-in-law of Sir James Douglas.**
>
> *(Reksten, Ill Hist BC p 85)*

THE SHIFT TO THE MAINLAND

The island dominated the BC government for three decades before the fast-growing population of the mainland eclipsed it. During this interval, provincial politics were plagued by scandal-ridden coalitions.

Inevitably, in the 1890s, Victoria yielded power to Vancouver, which had been forest only a decade before. By 1905, when the Canadian Pacific Railway acquired the Dunsmuirs' E&N Railway lands, BC's centre of gravity had shifted decisively away from Vancouver Island.

LOCAL GOVERNMENT

Local government followed the development of southeast Vancouver Island. The first to become a city was Victoria. It's the second oldest municipality in BC, after New Westminster — both incorporated in 1862. Next to incorporate was the farming district of North Cowichan (1873). The mining centre Nanaimo soon became a city (1874). After a period of development came two more: the mining village of Cumberland (1898) and the mining port of Ladysmith (1904).

The rugged Vancouver Island hinterland opened up ever more quickly, thanks to boats, trains and automobiles — but mostly to forestry. Many forestry-based communities came into being between the 1940s to the 1970s. As pop-

Did you know...

that in 1856 the smallest legislative assembly in British North America (seven members) was established on the Colony of Vancouver Island? About 40 people voted in this election.

ulation increased, regional district services (in the 1960s) and the unique Islands Trust (in 1974) evolved to meet the needs of present-day society.

Today there are 9 cities, 7 towns, 7 villages and 13 district municipalities on Vancouver Island. Many have their own fire and police departments besides other local services.

REGIONAL DISTRICT GOVERNMENTS

Each regional district has a board of directors whose members are nominated by municipal councils, and each municipality's population determines how many directors it has. Parts of the regional district that are not incorporated are called Electoral Areas, and their directors are appointed

Bio THE DUNSMUIRS

The Dunsmuirs were British Columbia's richest and most powerful family in the early years of the province. The dynasty built by the father and enlarged by the son dwindled to a mere trust fund by the third generation.

Robert Dunsmuir was born to mine coal — both his father and grandfather were managers of mines in Ayrshire, Scotland. Dunsmuir went to work in the Hudson's Bay Company's Fort Rupert mine in 1851, but before long his family was moved to Nanaimo, where the coal seams were extensive and of high quality.

Dunsmuir quickly proved the most knowledgeable miner on the island — and a canny businessman. In the 1870s he built the mining complex, town and port of Wellington-Departure Bay. His son James used the same model in developing large coal mining complexes in Cumberland-Union Bay and Extension-Ladysmith.

The Dunsmuirs were not noted for their attention to worker safety, a business decision that cost many lives. They further antagonized the European workforce by employing Asian workers at half wages and by their ruthless lock-outs and evictions from company-owned houses of striking miners. On the other hand, Robert's hands-on attitude and common touch made him a hero to many workers.

In the 1880s, the family fortune was fabulously enlarged by the by the province. The Nuu-Chah-Nulth Tribal Council nominates a director to the Alberni-Clayoquot board.

REGIONAL DISTRICT	MUNICIPALITIES	ELECTORAL AREAS	FIRST NATIONS
Alberni-Clayoquot	3	6	1
Capital	13	3	
Comox Valley	3	4	
Cowichan Valley	4	9	
Mt Waddington	4	4	
Nanaimo	4	7	
Strathcona	5	5	

(The Comox Valley and Strathcona Regional Districts were created from the Comox-Strathcona regional district in 2008.)

Esquimalt and Nanaimo Railway deal. Dunsmuir received a $750,000 subsidy and a huge grant of land — virtually the entire southeast quarter of the island — to construct the tiny line. Robert took up politics, moved with his large family to Victoria and built 39-room Craigdarroch Castle.

Robert Dunsmuir died at 63, his castle unfinished. His widow Joan administered the estate, while James ran the coal business and his brother Alexander, the E&N — on paper. In reality, Joan and James fought over the estate and became enemies. Alexander led a secret life and died in sordid circumstances in 1900, willing his estate to his brother, for which their mother sued James — her own son!

In his chequered political career, James resigned from the offices of both premier (1900-02) and lieutenant-governor (1906-09). James sold the E&N in 1905 and divested the coal business in 1910. His large family lived in untrammeled luxury in Hatley Park, their 250-hectare Colwood estate.

James never recovered from the grief of losing his younger son, who was aboard the *Lusitania* when it was torpedoed in 1915. He died in 1920, leaving his surviving siblings and nine children to spend the family fortune.

Take 5 FIVE POLITICAL EVENTS
THAT CHANGED THE ISLAND

1. **The Pig War:** The Hudson's Bay Company (HBC) had a sheep farm on San Juan Island when, in 1859, some Americans settled nearby, and one of them shot a pig belonging to an HBC employee. A dispute erupted over compensation. A US Army detachment arrived, to be countered by two British warships. The arming continued through the summer of 1859, to the point where there were 461 American troops facing off against five warships carrying more than 2,100 men. James Douglas urged Admiral Baynes to attack, but common sense prevailed. Diplomacy led to joint military occupation of the island. In 1872, an international commission gave all the San Juan Islands to the USA. The Union Jack still flies above the British Camp, raised and lowered daily by Americans.

2. **First Nations Resource Use:** The traditional fishery of the Cowichan First Nation was based on the construction of between 15 and 21 weirs along the Cowichan River. By 1878, however, the government made it illegal to use nets to catch salmon in fresh water. The Aboriginal food fishery was curtailed to promote the commercial fishery.

Fisheries officers charged offenders and removed the weirs. The Cowichan First Nation hired a Victoria lawyer to fight charges brought against one aboriginal fisher. The charges were dismissed — the weirs did not prevent salmon from reaching their spawning grounds. (The logging industry, meanwhile, was using the river to run logs to tidewater. Log jams and the resulting alteration of river channels caused the erosion of some 117 acres of Cowichan Indian Reserve land between 1878 and 1892.)

3. **The Sealing Ban:** Every spring some 60 schooners left Victoria with First Nations hunters in search of seal herds migrating across the open Pacific Ocean. Some Canadian sealers attracted diplomatic outrage for stealing pelts at gunpoint. But it was the shrinking seal population that made Canada the butt of the first international environmental protest, starting in 1891. By 1911, a treaty signed by the USA, Russia, Japan and the United Kingdom banned the hunt and left Canada out in the cold. As the sun set on Vancouver Island's sealing industry, the US government agreed to pay Canadian sealers compensation. A commission in Victoria registered 1,600 claims totaling $9 million. The US paid $200,000.

4. **The Great Strike, 1912-14:** Between 1884 and 1912, 373 men died from mine explosions alone on Vancouver Island. When a group of Extension miners reported unsafe conditions in 1912, the company

simply fired them. Miners in Cumberland responded by staging a one-day strike. The company responded by locking out 2,000 men and required each miner to sign a 2-year contract.

The company pressured miners into signing the contract, threw striking workers and their families out of their homes, and lured strike-breaking miners from England. Some strikers lived in tents that winter. The Extension mine was worked by scabs, and so, by the following spring, were most of the big Nanaimo mines. Plainclothed Provincial Police "specials" provoked confrontations. The hatred escalated until, on August 13, strikers went from home to home in Ladysmith, smashing windows and intimidating strikebreakers. In Extension, strikers barricaded the mine, trashed its Chinatown and torched scabs' home.

The strikebreakers and their families fled into the bush. The militia took charge in Nanaimo, Ladysmith and Cumberland, arresting 213 strikers (but not one strikebreaker) and kept the peace. After the United Mine Workers of America withdrew its support in July 1914, the strike dragged on until after the outbreak of war in Europe in August, when the strikers capitulated. So ended the biggest political conflict in the island's history.

5. **Forest workers organize:** In the 20s and 30s, the heyday of railway logging, high-speed cable yarding rigs were extremely dangerous. The loss of life was staggering: 50 loggers died at one site near Campbell River. The struggle for collective bargaining began slowly. Union organizers were not welcome in logging camps. Goons turfed them out, and the bosses kept a blacklist. As wages fell in the Great Depression, the forest workers took more determined action. In January 1934, 64 men were fired at a Bloedel, Stewart and Welch (BS&W) camp. A sympathy strike spread to other camps in the area and became a coast-wide shutdown, with public opinion swinging toward the strikers. BS&W imported strikebreakers and reopened its Great Central Lake camp, whereupon 500 strikers trekked from Parksville to protest. The strike ended when the BC government raised the workers' minimum wage, but the work of organizing continued in the sawmills. Finally, in 1937, provincial legislation recognized the workers' right to join unions. When the local Lumber Workers' Union merged with the International Woodworkers of America (IWA), forestry workers found a powerful ally.

THE ISLANDS TRUST

The Islands Trust is a federation of local governments established in 1974 to provide land-use planning and development control over 13 major islands and more than 450 smaller islands in the Gulf Islands and Howe Sound. Within an area of 5,200 km² (including land and water) where about 23,000 people live, the Trust is governed by 26 elected trustees from 12 local trust areas and the district municipality of Bowen Island.

LOCAL POLITICS

Vancouver Island's urban centres tend to vote "left" while farming communities and affluent suburbs vote "right." Provincially, the islands regularly elect more NDP than Liberal MLAs.

Islanders also have a streak of grassroots activism. The largest act of civil disobedience in Canada's history took place in Clayoquot Sound in 1993. Home-grown democrats exercise their right to be heard through a multitude of public forums. Do they carry any weight? There's a lively ongoing debate on the islands, as in other parts of Canada, about the state of our democratic institutions.

HOW THE ISLANDS VOTE

Federal Representation: The islands have six of BC's 36 seats in the House of Commons. Currently the NDP and the governing Conservative Party each hold three.

Provincial Representation: The islands have 13 of the 79 seats in BC's Legislative Assembly. The NDP currently holds nine, the governing Liberal Party four.

Did you know...

That First Nations people were able to vote in provincial elections only in 1949? And "status" First Nations people did not achieve the federal franchise until 1960.

ISLAND WOMEN IN POLITICS

1885: A women's suffrage petition is presented to the BC Legislature.

1895: Maria Grant is elected the first woman school trustee. She is the first women elected to such a position in Victoria and the province.

1917: BC women gain the right to vote in provincial elections.

1918: Mary Ellen Smith is elected as BC's first female Member of the Legislative Assembly.

1949: Nancy Hodges of Victoria becomes the first woman speaker of a provincial legislature and first in the British Commonwealth.

1953: May Campbell is the first Vancouver Island woman to run in a federal election, but is defeated.

1963: It is another ten years before another woman, Hazel Fee, tries for a federal seat.

1988: Lynn Hunter of the New Democratic Party wins her Saanich-Gulf Island seat and becomes the first Vancouver Island woman sent to Ottawa.

RACE RELATIONS

On Vancouver Island as elsewhere, there had always been an uneasy relationship between the British and Chinese. The white working class population felt the Chinese drove down wages and took their jobs, while employers like the Dunsmuirs took advantage of a disenfranchised labour force. Feelings became so strong that in 1878 the B.C.

Did you know...

that James Douglas was born in Guyana to a Scottish merchant and a free Creole — a woman of mixed black and white ancestry — from Barbados.

Did you know...

that Kim Campbell, the nineteenth Prime Minister of Canada, was born in Port Alberni? She is the only woman to have ever held this office.

legislature unanimously passed a bill stating Chinese should not be employed on the public works of the province.

Both the Chinese Head Tax and the Chinese Exclusion Act were federal responses to Vancouver Island demands. The first Chinese Head Tax was imposed in 1885 and was $50. It was later raised to $100 in 1900 and increased again in 1903 to $500.

Take 5 SID TAFLER'S FIVE MOST INTRIGUING ISLAND POLITICIANS

Sid Tafler is the author of *Us and Them: A Memoir of Tribes and Tribulations*, a book that explores what it means to be Canadian. As a Vancouver Island journalist and past editor of Victoria's alternative newsweekly, *Monday Magazine*, Tafler has interviewed many of Vancouver Island's leading and lesser political lights.

1. **Alan McKinnon:** He was the Progressive Conservative MP for Victoria for most of the '70s and well into the '80s. He was a decent man who believed in service. He served as minister of defence and minister of veterans' affairs in the Joe Clark government when I arrived in Victoria in late 1979. He believed the civil service in Ottawa undermined the Clark government and helped engineer its downfall. McKinnon represented the old, generally honourable PC party under people like Clark, David Crombie and Flora MacDonald. He detested Mulroney, who deposed Clark as party leader, and it turns out his judgment of Mulroney appears to be right.

2. **Peter Pollen, Mayor of Victoria:** Served as mayor from 1971-75 and again from 1981-85. He put his stamp on Victoria when he resisted the vertical growth that was common in most other cities at the time. Instead of highrises, Pollen wanted Victoria to maintain its charm. He helped preserve heritage buildings and focused on developing the inner harbour.

POTLATCH BAN

In 1884, the Government of Canada passed legislation known as the anti-potlatch law, which in effect banned all cultural practices for First Nations people in Canada. Despite the law, First Nations groups on Vancouver Island and elsewhere continued to secretly maintain their traditions. In 1921, the Kwakwaka'wakw people of Mamalilaculla held

3. **Charles Barber:** Charlie Barber was the perfect example of the emerging strength of the NDP. He was a brilliant, young politician who was knowledgeable on a wide range of topics. His skilful questions were devastating to the ruling Socreds during question period. He was also a founding member of Victoria's Cool Aid Society — a social organization that started providing services to the homeless in 1968.

4. **Dave Barrett:** Leader of the NDP and Premier of British Columbia for three years between 1972 and 1975. His party introduced question period and full Hansard transcripts to BC's legislative proceedings. He also formed the Agricultural Land Reserve and the Insurance Corporation of British Columbia. Barrett stayed on in Victoria after leaving provincial politics, later being elected the NDP Member of Parliament for Esquimalt.

5. **"Landslide" Al Passarell:** He was a northern MLA who looked like he stepped out of a Robert Service poem. In 1979, he defeated MLA Frank Calder by one vote, earning him the nickname of Landslide Al. Frank Calder and his wife were so confident they would defeat Passarell, they stayed in Victoria on election day. Passarell was a welcome breath of fresh air to the stuffy world of BC politics of the time. His wild demeanour made him one of many characters who made island politics interesting.

an illegal Potlatch. The result was 26 people were arrested for not renouncing their beliefs and giving up their ceremonial attire. The law was erased from the books in 1951 and potlatching continues to be central activity in First Nations culture.

The Island's Premiers

Of 33 premiers of BC since Confederation, only two — Simon Fraser Tolmie and Byron "Boss" Johnson — hailed from the island. Another 10 represented island ridings. The chart reveals the influence the island once had in provincial politics, and lost.

	PROFESSION	TERM	RIDING, PARTY (AFTER 1903)
John F. McCreight	Lawyer	1871-72	Victoria
Amor de Cosmos	Newspaper publisher	1872-74	Victoria
Robert Beaven	Businessman	1882-83	Victoria City
William Smithe	Farmer	1883-87	Cowichan
Theodore Davie	Lawyer	1892-95	Cowichan/Alberni
John H. Turner	Merchant	1895-98	Victoria City
James Dunsmuir	Businessman	1900-02	South Nanaimo
Edward G. Prior	Mining Engineer	1902-03	Victoria
Harlan C. Brewster	Cannery owner	1916-18	Alberni (Liberal)
Simon F. Tolmie	Agriculturist	1928-33	Victoria (Conservative)
John Hart	Businessman	1941-47	Victoria (Liberal/coalition)
Byron I. Johnson	Merchant	1947-52	Victoria (Liberal/coalition)

JAPANESE INTERNMENT

On February 26, 1942, the Canadian government began to expel "all persons of the Japanese racial origin" from a "protected area" within 160 km of the BC coast. For Vancouver Island and the Gulf Islands this meant hundreds of Japanese families had their homes and fishing boats seized and were forced to live in internment camps. They were not permitted to return to the coast until April 1949. By that time, all of their belongings were gone.

Weblinks

The Legislative Assembly of BC

www.leg.bc.ca.
History, visitor information and biographies.

Municipal websites

Budgets, profiles of the mayors and more:
www.victoria.ca
www.nanaimo.ca
www.city.port-alberni.bc.ca
www.city.courtenay.bc.ca

The Islands Trust

www.islandstrust.bc.ca
This regional democractic body has a large website describing its many activities in the Gulf Islands and others.

Did you know...

that BC's first 14 Premiers were non-partisan, meaning belong to no particular party? Richard McBride, in 1903, became the first partisan Premier, running as a Conservative.

Then and Now

Vancouver Island has undergone amazing transformations since the first European settlers arrived little more than 150 years ago.

The island's growth has been variable — now faster, now slower — but it's always been positive, as the decade-by-decade population summary shows. There's a boom-and-bust character to the region. Boom times connect the local economy with the larger world, and islanders have enjoyed their share of general prosperity, just as they've suffered their share of poverty during times of general depression.

VANCOUVER ISLAND POPULATION, THEN AND NOW

1881	17,292
1901	50,886
1921	108,792
1941	150,407
1961	290,835
1981	491,333
2001	664,451
2007	745,165

Sources: Statistics Canada and BC Statistics.

AGRICULTURE ON VANCOUVER ISLAND

Year	Total "improved" acres	Total farm population	Total number of farms
1931	56,880	14,877	4,061
1966	55,226	8,996	1,948
1971	54,313	NA	1,770
1981	63,646	NA	2,078

Sources: BC Statistics.

PACIFIC SALMON THEN AND NOW

The Pacific salmon is as much an icon for people on the west coast as the Northern cod is to people on the east. Unfortunately, similar to the cod, many of the seven native species of salmon in the waters around Vancouver Island are in distress.

Trouble began in the 1900's when poor logging practices and land clearing damaged the river sand streams where salmon begin and end their life journeys. Mining, agriculture, and urbanization added to the damage and simple overfishing caused many stocks to plummet and some to vanish. Global climate change presents a new threat.

The Department of Fisheries and Oceans has tried — more or less successfully, depending on who you talk to — to protect wild salmon stocks by limiting catches, operating hatcheries where salmon eggs are incubated, ensuring that fish farms comply with environmental regulations and even paying fishers not to fish, through a commercial license buy-back. Today, wild salmon continues to be caught but in much reduced numbers compared to even twenty years ago.

Source: David Suzuki Foundation.

Did you know...

that lightkeepers at the most remote lightstations start at the high end of the advertised pay scale, while lightkeepers at more easily accessible lightstations start lower on the pay scale?

BOB GRIFFIN'S FIVE MOST
MEANINGFUL PLACES ON VANCOUVER ISLAND

Dr. Robert Griffin manages the history section at the Royal BC Museum in Victoria. He joined the museum in 1979 and has co-curated several major exhibits, including *Rocks, Rigs, and Roughnecks* and *Whales: The Enduring Legacy*. He is also lead curator for *Free Spirit: Stories of You, Me and BC*, the museum's exhibition celebrating the 150th anniversary of the province. His main areas of study are British Columbia's mining and forest industries.

1. Underneath the streets of Nanaimo are the tunnels from where coal was extracted. I find it captivating to think about those mines as I drive the highways and streets, visualizing the hardships and hazards those miners faced underground.

2. As I drive near the Cowichan River I am always awestruck to think that here for about ten years near the turn of the century, loggers sent their logs down the river for sawmilling at Genoa Bay.

3. When travelling along either coast of Vancouver Island I find myself imaging all the activity that once existed, even though so little evidence remains. Each time I pass some isolated pilings jutting from the water's edge, I can see the ships loading their cases of salmon, perhaps at Kildonan, or smell the gagging stench from the pilchard reduction plants, maybe at CeePeeCee or Queen's Cove. Although little remains of Red Gap (Nanoose), a whole community stretched up the gulch from the Straits Lumber Company mill.

4. Piles of sawdust along Mill Bay sit under the water, disposed of by one of Vancouver Island's early sawmills. Drill sampling several years ago showed that a layer of sawdust from the mill covers over much of the floor of the inlet. That goes to show you the level of activity.

5. As I whip past Bamberton, heading up island, I can picture the cement that once hung like frozen drips over the hand rails, along the steps and even covering some buildings in the older and long abandoned parts of the former cement plant.

TIMELINE: DISASTERS ON VANCOUVER ISLAND

1875: Steamer *Pacific*, bound for San Francisco, collides with the *Orpheus* off Cape Flattery and sinks — more than 250 dead, with only two survivors; it is Victoria's worst maritime disaster ever.

1879: Fire and explosion in Dunsmuir's No. 1 Mine, Wellington — 11 men are killed.

1887: Explosion at the Vancouver Coal Company's No. 1 shaft in Nanaimo kills 147 workers and one rescuer.

1896: An overcrowded streetcar crashes through the Point Ellice Bridge in Victoria, killing 55 people, the worst streetcar accident in Canadian history.

1899: Fire destroys Cary Castle, the first Government House in Victoria.

1906: The *SS Valencia* strikes a reef on the west coast of Vancouver Island and sinks, drowning an estimated 136 people and prompting construction of the West Coast Lifesaving Trail, the Pachena Bay light and a Canadian Coast Guard station at Bamfield.

1910: Fire wipes out a block of stores on Government, Fort and Broad Streets in downtown Victoria, causing one and a half million dollars in damage.

1918: Magnitude 7 earthquake rocks the islands, with the greatest structural damage happening at the Estevan Point Lighthouse and an Ucluelet wharf.

1938: A huge forest fire known as the Bloedel Fire destroys 30,000 ha. between Campbell River and Courtenay.

1946: Earthquake of magnitude 7.3 damages buildings in Courtenay.

1947: A wildfire in the Nimkish Valley on the island's north end destroys 187 homes.

Did you know...

that Congregation Emanu-El is Canada's oldest synagogue in continuous use? It was completed in 1863 in Victoria in what was then the Colony of Vancouver Island and is today one of the city's oldest buildings.

Take 5 — FIVE BEST ARTIFACTS

FROM THE NANAIMO MUSEUM

In 2006, the Nanaimo District Museum initiated a creative fundraising campaign to help raise the $1.6 million needed to build a new museum that will be double the size of the old one. Staff picked the best artifacts in their collection and put them up for 'adoption.' The five items described below are staff favourites.

1. **Protection Mine Pocket Watch.** On September 19, 1918, Robert McArthur was wearing the watch when the Protection Island mine elevator cage he was in with 15 co-workers plummeted to the bottom of the shaft. When his body was recovered, the watch's crystal had broken and the hands had frozen at the time of impact, 7:10 a.m. The descendants of Robert McArthur 'adopted' this artifact as part of the museum's fundraising campaign.

2. **Princess Royal Teapot.** This beautiful clay teapot was brought from England onboard the Princess Royal in 1854.

3. **Apothecary Chest.** This chest was made in China around 1910 and brought to Nanaimo prior to World War I by Wong Kee (a.k.a. Wong Wah Soon) for use in his herbalist shop, Dai Song Tong, on 10 Pine Street. The chest was moved to the home of one of his daughters before the 1960 Chinatown fire.

4. **Bastion Cannon.** This cannon was cast at the Bailey & Pegg foundry in England. As it was common for merchant ships to carry arms, this cannon may have been used aboard an HBC ship before it was placed outside the historic Nanaimo Bastion.

5. **Frank Ney's Council Seat.** Frank Ney served as mayor of Nanaimo for twenty-one years. He was known for his outgoing personality and for playing a key role in initiating the annual Bathtub Race across Georgia Strait. He loved to dress up like a pirate at public events. This 1951 chair is marked with "Krug Furniture, Kitchener" and has a label stating the name of "Mayor Ney." It was transferred to the Nanaimo Museum from City Hall in 2003 when the Council Chamber chairs were replaced.

1951: 23 people are killed when their airplane hits Mount Benson near Nanaimo, the worst air disaster in Vancouver Island's history.

1957: Fire destroys the second Government house.

1960: Nanaimo's Chinatown is levelled by fire, leaving 250 people homeless, most of them elderly.

1963: An earthquake in Alaska creates a tidal wave in the Alberni Inlet, destroying or severely damaging 351 homes in Port Alberni.

1972: A freighter coming into Barkley Sound runs aground, spilling 400 tonnes of bunker oil and contaminating 19 km of coastline.

1977: Arsonist lights fire to the Imperial Oil tank farm in Nanaimo, killing himself and one firefighter.

1988: An oil tanker spills 5,500 barrels of oil off the coast of Oregon, contaminating the island's west coast, especially Tofino.

1998: A Russian trawler catches fire at the dockyard in Esquimalt. 200 people are evacuated.

2006: Fire engulfs Lumberworld in Saanich. Despite efforts by Saanich, Oak Bay, Esquimalt and Victoria firefighters, the building and inventory go up in smoke, at a cost of $6 million.

GETTIN' AROUND

Just over a century ago, horse and carriage, trains and boats were the main means by which Islanders traveled Vancouver Island. The introduction of the automobile, like it did elsewhere, changed forever the way Islanders traveled and how they viewed their lives.

Did you know...

that Vancouver Island is the home of Canada's last logging train? Today, Western Forest Products operates North America's longest running logging railway with 70 miles of track, 400 railcars and four diesel locomotives. The original steam locomotive, known as the "No. 113" has been retired, and is on show in the tiny community of Woss.

Approximately 80 percent of us still get to work in cars today. Our love affair with vehicles began in 1902 when Dr. E.C. Hart imported a two-seater that was "much admired" on the streets of Victoria, according to the *Victoria Daily Times*. In 2007 there were 510,000 vehicles registered on Vancouver Island.

BOATS

Is there a home on the Island that doesn't have a boat of some kind? Well, maybe a few, but living on an island surrounded by lots of little islands practically demands boat ownership, even if it's just a kayak.

The biggest boats, of course, are those owned by BC Ferries. The three newest ones coming into service in 2008 are the largest double-ended ferries in the world, capable of carrying 370 vehicles and 1,650 passengers. That's roughly three times the number of vehicles and twice the number of passengers that BC Ferries' first two vessels carried back in the 1960s.

TRAINS

As every schoolchild in British Columbia knows, BC agreed to join Canada if it could be connected by rail to the rest of the country. Residents of Vancouver Island expected the transcontinental railroad to end in Victoria, so they were more than just hugely disappointed when Prime Minister John A. Macdonald (he was also MP for Victoria at the time) decided the end of the line would be in Vancouver.

The Prime Minister, however, didn't forget about his constituents. He offered coal baron Robert Dunsmuir land and money to build a railroad (one that would also support his coal mines as well as a thriving lumber industry and the navy base in Esquimalt.) Construction began

Did you know...

that the Kinsol Trestle, the largest wooden railway trestle in the Commonwealth, was named for King Solomon's copper mine (abbreviated to Kinsol) which was abandoned in 1907?

on the Esquimalt & Nanaimo (E&N) railway in 1884 and the first section was finished two years later.

It was the Prime Minister himself who drove the last spike into the ground at Mile 25 (Cliffside) on the east side of Shawnigan Lake. The E&N was extended numerous times, and at its peak had 45 stations on its main line, eight on the Port Alberni Line and 36 on the Cowichan Line.

Back at the turn of the last century, short-distance train lines were essential because in many instances there were literally no roads. Three companies ran lines between Victoria and the Saanich Peninsula, with the last one being abandoned in 1935. CN ran passen-

Fore!

Hardship is often associated with the early days in Canadian history, but in Victoria at least the pursuit of pleasure was very much on the minds of some of the earliest settlers. For early English and Scottish settlers that pleasure came in the form of golf. As early as 1893, the Victoria Golf Club was created on the south-eastern tip of the island.

Good weather permitted year-round play, but in the early years the club was obliged to let cattle and sheep graze their fairways in the summer months. When the club expanded across Beach Drive in 1894, members had a new problem on their hands: how to land shots for two holes on the other side of the road without hitting people out for a stroll. A number of near-misses were documented, but club members insisted they had the right of way. This was finally resolved in 1923 when the club re-aligned its course to avoid the road.

Today, the Victoria Golf Course is Canada's oldest club still in its original location. You'll pay a lot more to join, however, than the $5 fee charged to the first patrons back in 1893. In 2008, the club's website noted that an active membership for one person costs $28,500 with monthly dues of $232 on top of that.

They Said It

> *"This problem is due to overproduction. There is only one solution. Let the Dominion issue a billion dollars of paper money and put the people to work."*
>
> **– Port Alberni Mayor J.A. Kendall speaking in 1931 as Island municipalities struggled with high unemployment in the early years of the Great Depression.**

ger trains ran twice daily to Milne's Landing near Sooke beginning in 1922 before ending in the 1960's.

CN tried to compete with the E&N by pushing a track from Victoria through to Port Alberni and on to Nootka Sound, but progress was slow and the company stopped laying tracks just past Youbou, although the right of way was completed almost to Port Alberni.

Today, the old CN right of way is part of the Trans-Canada bike trail, although the famous Kinsol Trestle, the largest wooden railway trestle in the British Commonwealth, is closed because of disrepair.

The E&N has survived under different owners (CP and RailAmerica) and in 2006 was donated to the Island Corridor Foundation, a non-profit group which contracts Southern Railway of Vancouver Island to operate the freight trains and provide crew for the daily Via Rail Canada passenger service from Victoria to Courtenay.

PLANES

Victoria has the distinction of being the site of Canada's first death involving an airplane. On August 6, 1913 an American barnstormer

Did you know...

that the last drive-in movie theatre on Vancouver Island was in Cassidy, near Nanaimo, and operated from 1952 until 1992?

by the name of John Bryant was killed when he crashed his Curtiss seaplane. Fifteen years later, in 1928, an even bigger tragedy unfolded when a Ford Tri-Motor flying from Victoria to Seattle crashed, killing all seven people aboard. It was Canada's first air disaster and it happened just a month after regular air service began at Lansdowne field in Greater Victoria, BC's first licensed airport.

Another first for Victoria — this time on a positive note — was the flight of the first all-Canadian aircraft. On September 8, 1910, William Gibson tested his 'twin-plane,' which had two wings, one behind the other, four bicycle wheels and a six-cylinder engine. Gibson's flight was short but successful. A couple weeks later he did it again, this time covering some 200 feet, much further than the Wright brothers managed at Kitty Hawk seven years earlier. Today, a plaque on Richmond Road marks the site of Gibson's historic flight.

By 1943, a new airport was created at Patricia Bay, site of today's Victoria International Airport. During World War II, 10,000 people trained at the Pat Bay base, the third largest aviation base in Canada. Other island communities with airports today are Nanaimo, Campbell River, Comox, Tofino, Qualicum Beach and Port Hardy.

Did you know...

that the oldest preserved Hudson's Bay Company fort in Canada is located in Nanaimo? The Bastion was built in 1853.

WIRED

Victoria was first on the island and first in BC to have street lighting. It all began in 1883 with a few arc lamps on top of tall poles powered by a 25-horsepower steam engine. In 1898, BC Electric built the first hydroelectric plant on the coast, near Victoria, but it took a long time for some of the more isolated communities to be hooked up to the grid. Tofino, for instance, didn't get electricity until 1951.

Sources: BC Hydro, Green Island Energy, and West Coast Environmental Law.

Campbell River's Loggers

The forest industry has been a mainstay of Vancouver Island's coastal communities. No surprise then that Campbell River holds the largest logging sports competition in Canada. Contestants come from Europe, Australia, New Zealand, the US and other parts of Canada to compete at hand bucking, axe throwing, standing block chop, log rolling and other feats of physical prowess involving logs.

North Island Logger Sports has become so popular that several TV channels film the events for broadcast in the US and Canada. For 2008, the prize pool topped $40,000.

The North Island Logger Sports Show
Is the place the loggers go
With sharpened saws to cut the block
Or climb the spar to reach the top
And some will try their birling skill
and get wet if they take a spill
Others will try the springboard chop
To be the best by the timers clock
Or be the one to take first place
In the axe throw or choker race
Lets mark the date so we're not late
For Logger Sports two thousand and eight

-Jim Lilburn

Source: Campbell River Salmon Society Website.

THE GREAT DEPRESSION

The Great Depression was difficult for many on Vancouver Island. Workers were laid off, wages were cut, and businesses slashed prices in an effort to stay open. In 1931, municipal mayors complained to the federal minister of labour that the number of men being laid off — 400 in Saanich, 250 in Cumberland and 300 in Port Alberni — was creating a crisis.

For those lucky enough to hang onto their jobs, deals could be had. According to a local newspaper report at the time, you could buy a 24-pound sack of Robin Hood flour for 63 cents at the Hudson's Bay store, a 1930 Chevrolet sedan for $650, or a family home in Oak Bay for $4,000.

ROYAL ROADS UNIVERSITY

Royal Roads University (RRU) occupies a 240-hectare resort of forests, gardens and Colwood oceanfront. At the heart of the innovative university is the castle that James Dunsmuir built for his family in 1908. In its day, it was the finest residence in Canada. The Dunsmuir family lived there until 1937.

The federal government acquired Hatley Park in 1940 and used it as a training centre for naval reservists. It evolved into a training centre for cadets, then a two-year military college. In the 1970s, Royal Roads

The Great Vancouver Fire

In July 1938, a fire that was quickly dubbed The Great Vancouver Island Fire, started in a huge piles of logs awaiting shipment northwest of Campbell River. From that small beginning, it roared south, narrowly missing Campbell River, but causing so much smoke on the highway that drivers had to turn on their headlights in daytime.

It didn't help matters that there had been a drought that summer and to make it all worse, there was lots of 'slash' — piles of tree tops and branches left behind by loggers — providing even more ready fuel. The magnitude of the fire was conveyed by *Vancouver Province* reporter Harold (Torchy) Anderson when he wrote, "Hundreds of men, scores of pumps, fifty miles of hose, snorting caterpillar bulldozers, axe and shovel crews — every available means of modern forest firefighting — is pitted against the red enemy."

A shipload of men, out of work due to the Depression, had been brought over from Vancouver to help fight the fire while two Navy destroyers stood by in case crews and local residents had to be evacuated. By the time the fire was stopped on the outskirts of Courtenay, almost three weeks after it began, it had burned through 30,000 hectares of logged and standing forests, costing the provincial government more than $400,000 in lost stumpage fees alone.

Military College became a full-fledged degree-granting institution.

The military college closed in 1995, and RRU opened with perhaps the most flexible curriculum in Canada, allowing students to combine work and study in Intenet-based learning, with brief stints of residence

Bio RODERICK HAIG-BROWN

Roderick Haig-Brown (1908-1976) escaped to North America after being expelled from a prestigious English prep school. He worked as a logger for six years before taking up writing. (His knowledge of logging shows in his novel *Timber*, called the best novel ever written about the subject.) In the Great Depression, he wrote, "Jobs were hard to get, and paid only enough to cover board and work clothes. So we made our own jobs, jacking logs off the beaches, setting out traps (fur prices held up well), trolling for salmon, even guiding occasional fishermen and hunters."

He married and settled in Campbell River to raise a family of four. In 1942, Haig-Brown was appointed a magistrate of the Provincial Court at Elkhorn, where he heard 200-300 criminal cases a year. He later served as chancellor of the University of Victoria and was a member of International Pacific Salmon Fisheries Commission.

Best-known as a writer about sport fishing, Haig-Brown had an intimate knowledge of Vancouver Island's back country which, married to a poetic sensibility, produced 23 books, including the classic memoirs *A River Never Sleeps* and *Measure of the Year*, and hundreds of magazine articles. In the process of addressing the causes of habitat loss — logging, mining, dams, pollution — he became the island's first outspoken conservationist. "The degradation of stream conditions," he wrote, "is almost certainly the greatest single factor in the decline of salmon and steelhead runs, and this reflects a colossal failure in land management, especially forest land management."

Today the former family home beside the Campbell River is operated as a bed-and-breakfast by the local museum.

at the university; or to pursue a one-year intensive degree program on campus. Students and staff get to smell the flowers in the extensive, well-tended gardens. There are guided tours, for a fee.

Weblinks

BC Archives
http://www.bcarchives.gov.bc.ca/index.htm
One of the major information sources about BC's human history, the BC Archives contains government documents and records; private historical manuscripts and papers; maps, charts and architectural plans; photographs; paintings, drawings and prints; audio and video tapes; film; newspapers; and an extensive library.

Encyclopedia of British Columbia
http://www.knowbc.com/index.asp
Everything you need to know about Canada's westernmost province. The BC Primer section includes milestones in BC's history, 100 best things about the province, and a quiz to test your knowledge.

Did you know...

that there are secret messages written in Morse code on some street signs on Broad Street in Victoria? Carved in granite are words like "bemused," "ghosts," and "just a moment."

Did you know...

that the Victoria and Esquimalt Telephone Company installed telephone poles and a line connecting Victoria and Esquimalt in 1880?

The First People

The First Nations of Vancouver Island are the inheritors of the ancient traditions of sea-going societies. They were societies shaped by the seasons and the natural and living world around them. The islands supported large First Nations populations — many times their present numbers.

Three groups each occupied a third of the island from time immemorial. The abundance of the land and sea was literally at their feet. Each of the groups developed its own society and culture, but have much in common.

These First Nations are today celebrated for their artistic achievements. Rich family cultural traditions have been preserved through the thinnest times. The connection with nature that the urbanized world has lost, First Nations people have at their fingertips. It is expressed in many ways — carving, weaving, myth and dance, to name a few.

After 150 years living on the margins of metropolitan society, First Nations are experiencing a revival and have reasserted their stake in the islands' natural resources.

FIRST NATIONS AND RESERVES

First Nations are autonomous groups that Canada's *Indian Act* calls bands. Their allotted lands are called reserves. A reserve is "a tract of land, the legal title to which is vested in Her Majesty, that has been set apart by Her Majesty for the use and benefit of a band."

The 2006 census lists 99 reserves, totalling less than 17,000 hectares and ranging in size from 2 to about 3,600 hectares, within Vancouver Island's 7 Regional Districts (which include parts of the mainland coast). Under the *Indian Act*, First Nations have elected band councils with many of the rights and prerogatives of local governments. Most First Nations have hereditary chiefs as well. In some, the hereditary chief is the ranking authority. In total there are about 28,000 people identifying themselves as First Nations within this region.

Source: Department of Justice and BC Statistics.

THE POPULATION

In Canada, the Aboriginal population comprises 3 groups: First Nations, Métis (people of both First Nations and European ancestry) and Inuit (people of the North). Canada has the second highest proportion of Aboriginal people of English-speaking countries on the Pacific Rim — more than the United States and Australia, and about one-quarter of that of New Zealand. In BC the proportion is higher; on Vancouver Island, higher still.

Proportion of Aboriginal to total population in:

Canada	3.8 percent
BC	4.8 percent
Vancouver Island and associated islands	5.75 percent

Source: Statistics Canada.

CULTURAL GROUPS

The Nuu-Chah-Nulth inhabit the west coast between Cape Cook and east of Port San Juan. There are about 8,500 registered members in 14 nations. The biggest centres are Marktosis, on Flores Island, and

Tsahaheh, near Port Alberni.

The Ditidaht and Pecheedaht First Nations (706 and 259 registered members in 2007) maintain separate identities. Their territories are on the southwest coast, between the Nuu-Chah-Nulth and Salish areas.

The Coast Salish occupy the Gulf Islands and southeastern Vancouver Island as far north as Quadra Island, the mainland coast as far north as Bute Inlet, east as far as the Fraser Canyon (where the traditional territories of Coast and Interior Salish nations divide) and in northwest Washington, USA. There are about 12,300 members in 19 nations on the islands. Main centres include Cowichan, Nanaimo, Chemainus, and Victoria.

The Kwakwaka'wakw (kwa-kwa-keea-wak) occupy the east coast of Vancouver Island from Campbell River north, the west coast north of Cape Cook, and the mainland coast as far north as Smith Sound. There are about 4,400 registered members in eight nations on Vancouver Island and surrounding areas. Their main centres are Tsulquate, near Port Hardy, Alert Bay on Cormorant Island, and Campbell River.

Source: Department of Indian Affairs and Northern Development.

TRADITIONAL SOCIETY

First Nations have traditionally lived in salt-water villages and followed a seasonal round of fishing, gathering, hunting and, in winter, feasting.

Although science and research have begun to contribute to understanding First Nations societies, much of what we know about their traditional societies comes from First Nations people themselves.

First Nations had well-developed concepts of ownership and inher-

Did you know...

that First Nations people of Vancouver Island who speak Nuu-Chah-Nulth were long called the Nootka? *The Handbook of the North American Indians*, published in 1992, refers to these peoples as Nootkans. Nuu-Chah-Nulth is the name in common use today.

Take 5 — FIRST NATIONS CULTURAL CENTRES AND MUSEUMS

1. **I-Hos Gallery**, 3310 Comox Road, Courtenay
2. **Nuyumbalees Cultural Centre**, We Wai Kai (Cape Mudge) Village, Quadra Island
3. **Quw'utsun' Cultural and Conference Centre**, 200 Cowichan Way, Duncan
4. **Royal BC Museum**, Belleville Street, Victoria
5. **U'mista Cultural Centre**, Alert Bay, Cormorant Island

itance. Ownership included rights (the right of a family to fish a certain river). It included privileges (where one sits at feasts). It included powers (the power to compel visitors to observe a certain ritual before being allowed to land a boat).

Ownership of lands and waters was held by the leading families. Local rights to resources were more widely held. Each nation's territories were governed by a tightly-woven complex of rights. Ownership was usually transferred in a public ceremony and inheritances memorialized in the oral record. Outsiders occasionally came into temporary rights by marriage.

FOOD-GATHERING

During the food-gathering season, communities dispersed into smaller groups. Members of the Saanich First Nation on southern Vancouver Island had fishing rights near Tsawwassen (near the Fraser River) during the salmon runs. The fishing fleet travelled across the Strait of Georgia and fished alongside those from other First Nations. The men stayed in a camp on the beach at Tsawwassen, while at the same time the women might be gathering berries, grasses for weaving, roots, bulbs, medicinal plants, and shellfish. Nuu-Chah-Nulth First Nations maintained summer villages near the open ocean where they could go whaling and fish for halibut.

WINTER VILLAGES

When the weather turned stormy around the month of November, all would gather at a large central location for the winter. Winter villages were situated in areas protected from prevailing winds. A village might

Take 5 NANCY TURNER'S MOST USEFUL NATIVE PLANTS

Nancy Turner is a world-renowned authority on traditional plant and environmental knowledge (ethnobotany). She is a distinguished professor in the school of Environmental Studies at the University of Victoria and author of *The Earth's Blanket: Traditional Teachings for Sustainable Living* (2005) and many other books. She has lived on Vancouver Island for 55 years.

1. **Western red cedar:** Cedar has been important for First Nations people in every way — to get around, for shelter, fuel, clothing, basketry, bent-wood boxes and so much more — it's an icon.

2. **Salal:** The sweet, juicy berries can be cooked and dried in cakes. It was very important in the past to be able to dry food to survive in the winter. Salal leaves are also used for flavouring in pit cooking.

3. **Red alder:** Alder bark is an important traditional medicine — it has antibiotic properties and has been used to treat tuberculosis, stomach ailments and skin problems. Alder wood is the fuel of choice for smoking fish. The wood can be used for carving masks and bowls. The cambium is edible. Alder is an important pioneer tree that adds nitrogen to the soil.

4. **Sword fern:** These ferns are important in traditional winter ceremonies — as a bed for salmon in the first-salmon ceremony, and as part of the costumes of dancers. Some people have also used them in pit cooking. They are an important part of the understorey in many parts of the island.

5. **Springbank clover:** Our native perennial clover is found in river estuaries and tidal marshes along the coast. First Nations people valued it as a nutritious root vegetable — they ate the white rhizomes — and tended clover patches like gardens. Clover Point, in Victoria, was named after this plant.

have three rows of big houses, and the Chiefs occupied the best sites.

The big houses of the Nuu-chah-nulth were depicted in famous engravings by John Webber, who accompanied Cook on his visit to Nootka Sound in 1778. Mammoth houseposts, with animated faces carved into the wood, supported huge log beams. The whole building was clad in huge square cedar shakes. The inside interior space might measure 20 m by 20 m. The big house provided living space for all the Chief's relations and room for many visitors during winter ceremonies and other special occasions. The fire pit formed a focal point and some Kwakwaka'wakw houses were banked in tiers. The roof shakes could be moved to let smoke escape.

The winter ceremonials of the Kwakwaka'wakw were described in great detail in the 1800s by the anthropologist Franz Boas. Conspicuous feasting was accompanied by speeches of praise or boast-

Bio MAQUINNA HATS

A famous portrait of Chief Maquinna dates from 1791. The picture was engraved by Spanish artist Tomás de Suría, who visited Nootka on Alejandro Malaspina's expedition. The young chief with the thin moustache posed in a conical hat of tightly woven fibre, with an elegant bulb on top. The artist captured the graphic detail on the sides of the hat — human figures with harpoons standing at the bows of two canoes, each chasing a whale. Such decoration was emblematic of high estate.

Nearly 20 of these whaler hats have survived from the 18th century. One method of construction was to weave split spruce roots together with dyed cedar bark, overlaid with light-toned marine grass. There were two layers of weaving and a tight-fitting cap inside. Woven basketry-hats are a distinctive craft transmitted through generations of Nuu-Chah-Nulth women.

Today, so-called Maquinna hats are prized by collectors. For a hat of traditional design by the famed Ahousaht weaver Jessie Webster, expect to pay about $9,000 at House of Himwitsa in Tofino. A contemporary hat sells for $3,450 at I-Hos Gallery in Courtenay.

They Said It

> "... in the evening, several of the larger Canoes saluted us, by making a Circuit around the ships and giving 3 Halloos at their departure. They paddle in most excellent time, the foremost man every 3rd or 4th Stroke making flourishes with his paddle. The halloo is a single note in which they all join, swelling it out in the middle and letting the sound die away in a Calm with the hills around us. It had an effect infinitely superior to what might be imagined from any thing so simple."
>
> **– Lieut. James Burney, aboard HMS Discovery, in Nootka Sound March 30, 1778.**

ing, elaborate theatrical productions in costume, masks and props, dancing and drumming. They would go on for days. The young people would be initiated into secret societies during this season.

THE SALISH SEA

Most people know the inland basin of the Pacific Ocean between Vancouver Island and the mainland as the Strait of Georgia. The name Salish Sea started to appear in the local vocabulary in the 1980s and has gained wide usage. A member of the Chemainus First Nation recently proposed that Georgia Strait be renamed the Salish Sea, something the provincial government agreed to consider.

Ancient remains unearthed (dated by scientific analysis) and pieced together into a sequence tell the story of the migration of Salish people to the Pacific coast. The earliest Salish burial sites and remains of tools and middens in the Fraser Valley and on the shores of the Salish Sea are about 3,200 years old. Artifacts have been found in the Salish heartland, in the Fraser Canyon and further north, which suggest a linkage with the people of the coast.

THEY CALLED IT NOOTKA

Yuquot was the summer village of the Mowachaht First Nation and their chief Maquinna was the owner of all the rivers flowing into Tlupana and Tahsis inlets and half of Nootka Island. Maquinna's coun-

They Said It

sel commonly prevailed. He was first among equals, having formed alliances with the chiefs of neighbouring nations. His successors are called Maquinna to this day.

It was into Nootka Sound on March 30, 1778 that James Cook's two ships steered with a damaged mast and water in short supply after a month of bad weather.

Just inside the entrance they encountered the teeming village. Canoes full of people came out to welcome their ships. *Itchme nootka*, they called — "go around the harbour." *Nootka* means "go around" in Nuu-Chah-Nulth. Cook's men thought they said they were the Nootka people. The name stuck.

Cook's two ships spent a month anchored off Yuquot, in Friendly Cove, while his men felled a giant Douglas fir, floated it back, fitted it to the *Resolution* and rerigged the mizzen. Maquinna made friends with the English, gave them the freedom of the place, and invited them into the big houses of Yuquot. On maps published after Cook's voyage, Nootka was the only place between California and Alaska.

Did you know...

that an ancient shell midden at Bear Cove, near Port Hardy on northeastern Vancouver Island, was found to have stone tools underneath it that were carbon-dated to approximately 8,000 years ago? The tools include flat stones flaked to create sharp edges — perhaps for scraping skins. It's among the oldest evidence of human presence on the island.

BENTWOOD BOX COOKING

One versatile First Nations invention is a watertight wooden box made without glue, nails or screws. The four sides are a single plank, typically of cedar, that is kerfed — notched across the plank to make it easy to bend in three places — and steamed until pliable. The ends meet and are sewn together with cedar roots or pegged. The top and bottom are made snugly to overlap the sides.

Many bentwood boxes were made large enough to store clothing and ceremonial regalia. They could also be used to store perishables. One early Vancouver Island observer reported that a bentwood box holding eulachon oil required two men to lift it.

Bentwood box cooking is Canada's only truly indigenous cooking

No Carbs

The traditional diet of First Nations did not include much starch or sugar. They derived most of their calories from protein and fats, especially from fish and other seafood. After contact, however, came a diet heavy on carbohydrates and refined sugars, which have been devastating for First Nations people, whose metabolism is different from the European in essential ways. Among those who have adapted to the world of fast food, the incidence of diabetes is three to five times higher than in the general population. The risks associated with untreated diabetes are grim — kidney failure, amputation, heart attack. It's nothing less than a public health emergency and treatment costs are enormous.

Dr. Jay Wortman, a physician of First Nations ancestry, discovered he had diabetes in his 50s. When he deleted carbs and sugar from his diet, his blood sugar dropped and he lost weight. To find out whether the no-carb diet worked for other First Nations people, Dr. Wortman secured Health Canada research funds, put together a team and enlisted members of the Namgis First Nation in Alert Bay to take the no-carb challenge. The struggle of 100 recruits to maintain the diet for a year, monitored by a local physician and nurse, is chronicled in My Big, Fat Diet, a one-hour documentary that aired on CBC in 2008.

technique, says Anita Stewart, a scholar of Canadian cuisine. The technology was used all over the island. Indeed bentwood box cooking by First Nations women of Yuquot was described as early as 1778 by Captain Cook in his journals.

A box is filled with water and put beside the fire pit, where small stones are placed to heat them. When the stones are ready the cook puts the raw food into the box and adds hot stones. The water quickly comes to a boil. The process continues until the food is cooked.

Today a carved and painted 11"x11"x16" bentwood box by Kwakwaka'wakw artist Bruce Alfred sells for approximately $4,000 at Spirits of the West Coast Art Gallery in Courtenay.

TECHNOLOGIES FOR FOOD GATHERING

Nuu-Chah-Nulth have a thousand uses for the life forms of the seashore, a thousand for those of the forest. To catch the bounty, they would use appropriate technologies. In herring spawning season, cut a hemlock sapling, invert it in the water, wait for a tide, remove — the needles will be bright orange with herring roe. To carry the goods, many ingenious containers evolved. One example of that is the shoulder-strapped oyster carry-bag made of woven spruce roots.

SALISH TEXTILES

Traditional Salish weaving used dog hair or mountain goat hair. The Cowichan First Nation raised wool dogs (now extinct); they combed the hair out with knives. Mountain goat hair they obtained by trade with mainland First Nations.

To make yarn they used hand-turned spindles, unique to the area, fitted with disks of wood or bone. The disk, known as a spindle whorl, helps keep the spindle spinning and the wool in place as it is spun. Whorls were embellished with carvings of people or animals or geometric shapes, some representing the machine's power to transform "wool into wealth." Watching the spinning shapes blur, the operator would fall into a trance. This essential step is, Salish people believe, a way of imbuing the textile with power.

Salish women weavers used a 2-bar loom with a continuous warp. Besides blankets and robes and other useful products of their work, they wove large 4 m^2 blankets that were used solely as symbols of wealth.

Toronto artist Paul Kane, on Vancouver Island in 1847, sketched and painted Salish women spinning yarn and weaving blankets. Today, carved spindle whorls are appreciated as icons of the Coast Salish people's cultural richness.

Camas Agriculture

Cheryl Bryce, land manager of the Songhees First Nation, welcomes visitors to the Matson Lands, a conservation area on the Esquimalt waterfront, near downtown Victoria. In the shadow of a high-rise apartment building grow gnarled oak trees, flushed with spring leaves. Under them, a meadow of scattered large blue six-pointed camas flowers. The one-hectare site was donated by the building's developer, Mandalay Developments Ltd., and is under the protection of the Habitat Acquisition Trust of BC.

The Songhees First Nation is interested in the site because it is a rare remnant Garry oak meadow. Traditional Salish communities within the Garry oak ecosystem used such meadows for sustainable agriculture. Women tended family-owned camas patches. They prepared the sites by burning the grass. They weeded out the deadly white-flowered death camas. In spring and summer they harvested the camas bulbs.

Bryce brandishes an arm-long digging stick, with which she digs up a camas plant, unearthing a yellow bulb. Camas bulbs make a moderately-nutritious foodstuff. Easier to digest than potatoes, camas makes a good substitute as a starchy side dish.

One traditional way of cooking was to steam the bulbs until soft, pound and make them into cakes, which would be dried and stored for winter use. Made into flour, it could be added to soups, stews and salads.

COWICHAN SWEATERS

Salish women learned knitting after settlers came to the Cowichan valley in 1862. History records that, Sister Marie-Angèle of the Quamichan mission of the Sisters of St. Ann was the teacher. The knitters began using wool from the settlers' sheep to knit thick pullover sweaters that turned the rain.

The process and the products are the same today. In washing the wool, the crafter takes care to ensure the natural oils remain in the fibres, keeping the product waterproof. They card, comb and spin the wool by hand. They use combinations of white, brown, grey and black wool, relying on natural tones, not dyes, to create the familiar animal designs, framed by distinctive bands of geometric shapes. Cowichan sweaters are knit "in the round" so that the only seams are in the shoulders. The combination of untreated wool and seamless knitting make the sweaters extremely durable.

Non-Aboriginal knitters long ago picked up the design and began producing knock-offs with sporting motifs — curling stones and fishing rods. Commercial imitations also began to appear and recently the look of the Cowichan sweater has found favour in the world of fashion: The Gap sells sweaters of Cowichan-inspired design, and Calvin Klein recently marketed a silk and mohair line.

To protect their unique product against imitation, the Salish community began to certify it. There's a label on an authentic Cowichan sweater that guarantees it hand-knit from undyed, hand-spun wool.

It's wearable art. Adult sweaters begin at over $200. The

Did you know...

that people were thought to have lived on offshore islands during the last glaciation about 15,000 years ago? Underwater archeology has discovered human evidence on seamounts more than 100 m below the present sea level not far off the coast of Vancouver Island. It's possible that the earliest Aboriginal people on this coast adapted to living amid sea ice by hunting large sea mammals.

Qu'wutsun' Cultural Centre in Duncan sells Cowichan sweaters made to measure. Antique sweaters are displayed in the gift shop. The community of sweater-makers was featured in the 2000 film, "The Story of the Coast Salish Knitters."

CEDAR

Traditional economies were founded on western red cedar. The moisture-loving conifer is plentiful on the wet west coast. Its light, strong wood is easily shaped for shelter, utensils, transportation, storage and cooking. Biochemistry also makes cedar resist rot and infestation. The bark can be peeled off the trunk of the standing tree in lengths, then woven into clothing, bags, sails, even hats. Among its many uses, the most widely known are the Kwakwaka'wakw ceremonial (totem) poles, canoes, big houses, and masks.

CANOES

All of Vancouver Island's First Nations made canoes of dug-out cedar. Indeed canoes were mainstays of the economy. The traditional technique for obtaining wood for a canoe was to slab off a large chunk of a much larger tree, using wedges. The biggest cargo canoes were 20 m long and the Nuu-Chah-Nulth have a long and proud history of whaling in canoes.

Today, the art of canoe-making is enjoying a revival in the Tla-o-qui-aht First Nation. Joe Martin runs a successful industry based in Opitsaht and Tofino. He has carved some 25 canoes, including a whaling canoe for the Makah First Nation in Washington.

Canoe travel is the focus of Tlaook Cultural Adventures. Based in Clayoquot Sound and operated by Joe Martin's daughter Gisele, Tlaook offers an all-day adventure, paddling a traditional dugout canoe from Tofino to Echachis Island and back, with a salmon barbecue on the beach.

Canoes have also been vehicles of healing. Artist Roy Henry Vickers organized the famous 2,500 km VisionQuest paddle from the Skeena River to Victoria in 1987. Together with the RCMP, First Nations people undertook the mammoth trip to raise money for an alcohol treatment centre on Vancouver Island.

POPULATION LOSS

Disease stalked First Nations before and after European settlement. The small pox epidemic of 1862 devastated coastal populations. The losses hit some nations harder than others:

	POPULATION BEFORE	POPULATION LOSS
Kwakiutl	7,650	69 percent
Comox	1,080	53 percent
Songhees, Saanich	1,050	46 percent

Source: Handbook of the North American Indians.

TREATIES, RESERVES, LAND CLAIMS

When Vancouver Island became a colony in 1849, James Douglas began to approach First Nations leaders proposing to buy their lands for the British Crown. Between 1850 and 1854 (no treaties were made after 1854) he concluded 14 such purchases — 13 with Songhees, Esquimalt, Saanich, Clallam, Sooke and Snuneymew (Nanaimo) First Nations of the Salish, and the last with the Kwakiutl First Nation of the Kwakwaka'wakw. First Nations surrendered title to their traditional lands forever, but could continue to hunt and fish on them.

Following British Columbia joining the Canadian Confederation in 1871, a system of reserves was established under federal authority and lands transferred from the province.

First Nations in BC were allotted a small fraction of the area per person given to settlers who preempted land, lived on it, logged and farmed it. First Nations were prevented from preempting land.

Almost at once, First Nations lodged protests, claiming they never surrendered or sold their lands and thus should be compensated for the loss. A Cowichan Chief joined a delegation that gained an audience with King Edward VII in 1906. The monarch gave them a sympathetic hearing that amounted to nothing. For decades the BC Government simply pretended that Aboriginal title did not exist — or that, if it once had existed, it was extinguished.

Politically disenfranchised and economically dependent, First Nations kept trying to get a fair hearing for their land claims. In the 1970s the courts began to interpret the law in their favour.

It was only after the Oka Crisis, when Aboriginal anger spilled out into the streets, that the BC Government agreed to negotiate treaties that involve First Nations land claims.

The first such claim to be settled was that of the Nisgaa Nation in 2000.

Only two have been signed since — one on Vancouver Island. Under the Maa-Nulth Treaty of 2007, 5 Nuu-Chah-Nulth nations will get title to their reserves.

RECENT HISTORY

- 1990: Manitoba First Nations MLA Elijah Harper helps kill the Meech Lake Accord; Blockade and armed confrontation in Kanesatake, Quebec — the Oka crisis and the BC Government agrees to negotiate land claims.
- 1991: Royal Commission on Aboriginal Peoples establish Delgaamukw judgment by Chief Justice Allen McEachern, BC Supreme Court, in Gitksan-Wet'sueten land claim suit.
- 1993: Delgamuukw decision reversed in BC Court of Appeal.
- 1995: Blockade and armed confrontation at Gustavson Lake, BC.
- 1996: Report of the Royal Commission on Aboriginal Peoples.

They Said It

"… it is just and reasonable, and essential to our Interest, and the Security of our Colonies, that the several Nations or Tribes of Indians with whom We are connected, and who live under our Protection, should not be molested or disturbed in the Possession of such Parts of Our Dominions and Territories as, not having been ceded to or purchased by Us, are reserved to them, or any of them, as their Hunting Grounds …"

– **The Royal Proclamation of October 7, 1763**, which has been called the *Magna Carta* of First Peoples' rights.

- 2000: Nisgaa Nation Treaty — first on BC coast in 150 years.
- 2002: First Nations and the BC Government start making child welfare a First Nations responsibility.
- 2004: Aboriginal roundtable with federal cabinet ministers set the stage for the beginning of the implementation of royal commission recommendations.
- 2005: BC Government announces a "new relationship" with Aboriginal peoples.
- First Ministers Conference on Aboriginal Affairs — the Kelowna Accord — brings the roundtable process to the point of action — but 10 days later the Liberals lose the federal election and the Kelowna Accord is shelved.
- 2006: 10-year report card on Royal Commission progress by Assembly of First Nations. Canada's governments are graded for progress in 66 areas; number of those areas in which Canada received an A: one; number of those areas that receive an F: 37
- 2007: Tsawwassen and Maa-Nulth First Nations treaties — Maa-Nulth the first on Vancouver Island; First Nations communities are now deeply divided over treaty negotiations.
- 2008: Canada's prime minister apologizes for abuses of First Nations children in residential schools; Truth and Reconciliation Commission begins hearings throughout BC.

Weblinks

BC Archives
http://www.bcarchives.gov.bc.ca/
Hundreds of historical photos of First Nations in a searchable database.

Songhees First Nation
http://www.songheesnation.com/html/chiefs.htm
A robust website with a large and interesting section on Land Management.